SQL: Step-by-Step

SQL: Step-by-Step

F. D. Rolland

Department of Computing
Manchester Metropolitan University

INTERNATIONAL THOMSON COMPUTER PRESS

I(T)P An International Thomson Publishing Company

London • Bonn • Boston • Johannesburg • Madrid • Melbourne • Mexico City • New York • Paris
Singapore • Tokyo • Toronto • Albany, NY • Belmont, CA • Cincinnati, OH • Detroit, MI

SQL: Step-by-Step
Copyright © 1996 International Thomson Computer Press

I T P A division of International Thomson Publishing Inc.
The ITP logo is a trademark under licence.

For more information, contact:

International Thomson Computer Press
Berkshire House
168–173 High Holborn
London WC1V 7AA
UK

International Thomson Computer Press
20 Park Plaza
Suite 1001
Boston, MA 02116
USA

Imprints of International Thomson Publishing

International Thomson Publishing GmbH
Königswinterer Straße 418
53227 Bonn
Germany

International Thomson Publishing Asia
221 Henderson Road #05–10
Henderson Building
Singapore 0315

Thomas Nelson Australia
102 Dodds Street
South Melbourne, 3205
Victoria
Australia

International Thomson Publishing Japan
Hirakawacho Kyowa Building, 3F
2–2–1 Hirakawacho
Chiyoda-ku, 102 Tokyo
Japan

Nelson Canada
1120 Birchmount Road
Scarborough, Ontario
Canada M1K 5G4

International Thomson Editores
Campos Eliseos 385, Piso 7
Col. Polenco
11560 Mexico D. F. Mexico

International Thomson Publishing South Africa
PO Box 2459
Halfway House
1685 South Africa

International Thomson Publishing France
1, rue St. Georges
75 009 Paris
France

British Library Cataloguing-in-Publication Data
A catalogue record for this book is available from the British Library

Library of Congress Cataloging-in-Publication Data
A catalog record for this book is available from the Library of Congress

First Printed 1996

ISBN 1–85032–299–6

Commissioning Editor Samantha Whittaker
Cover Designed by Paragon International
Typeset by WestKey Limited, Falmouth, Cornwall
Printed in the UK by Clays Ltd, St Ives plc

Contents

Preface

This book aims at giving a simple, yet comprehensive, introduction to SQL (Structured Query Language). Its intended market is anyone who wants to learn to use SQL, be they students, academics, professional programmers, hobbyists or even end-users who would like to know more about their database system. By use of the index and appendices, it should also serve as a quick reference guide.

I have written the book in as informal a manner as possible without compromising technical precision. I hope that it is an entertaining as well as an informative read.

Why should anyone want to learn about SQL? The answer to this is that there is no more widely used language in the world of commercial computer databases. Major products such as DB2, ORACLE, Ingres, Informix and SyBase are completely SQL-based. Most other major database systems available provide an SQL interface. SQL knowledge is virtually mandatory for all serious users of databases.

SQL is first and foremost an interface for relational database systems. For this reason, I have included an introductory section on the basic principles of relational systems. This knowledge is vital in order to make sense of the language. The succeeding chapters take the reader through the process of building and manipulating databases using SQL. SQL has a series of well-defined international standards. Everything presented here conforms to the most recently published standard (SQL/92). The vast majority of the examples given in the text should work without amendment on all of the products listed above, and many others besides. Individual products will have their own extensions and features that are additional to the standard. There are no products currently available that implement the entire standard. Those parts of the language that are hardly ever supported are deliberately separated out into a chapter on their own. My aim is to produce a text that is as universally useful as possible.

I have also included a chapter on possible future directions for SQL. I hope that the casual reader finds this interesting in its own right.

1 | Before getting started with SQL

▨ 1.1 SQL and relational databases

SQL ('Structured Query Language') is the foremost database language of today. Nearly every available database product is either built around SQL or supplies an SQL interface. SQL knowledge is vital for all those who are seriously interested in databases, be they professional database developers, academics or students.

Why is SQL so dominant? Here are some answers.

- **Ease of use.** SQL is a relatively simple language to learn. With just a small amount of knowledge, the user can build and manipulate quite large and complex databases.
- **Standardisation.** SQL has a series of well-defined international standards. Most of the SQL that a database user has learned for one particular product can usually be transferred directly to another SQL product. Thanks to standardization, software transfer between different SQL-based products is usually achievable. This is not to say that all SQLs are the same. However, the vast majority of SQLs take the form of extensions

around the international standard. Remove the extensions from the code and one is left with an SQL program that will run with minimal amendment on any SQL platform.

- **The relational platform.** SQL was developed as a language specifically for use with relational database systems. The relational approach to database management has gradually gained widespread acceptance and is now pre-dominant amongst vendors of packaged database systems. The majority of the earliest and most successful relational database vendors built their systems around SQL. Nearly all other relational database suppliers have since found it necessary to provide an SQL interface to their products in order to survive in the marketplace. SQL interfaces are also supplied by suppliers of non-relational products, such is the user demand.

This is not to suggest that an SQL-based relational database is a panacea for all database requirements. Relational databases have been found to be severely limited when applied to fields beyond the traditional data storage requirements of a business organization. Areas such as graphics databases, multimedia databases, geographic databases and knowledge bases all require facilities that do not rest easily on a relational platform. Most leading-edge database research these days is into models that are more appropriate to these new forms of database. However, the power of the SQL presence is shown by the fact that many of the newly proposed models for database modelling include an extended form of SQL appropriate for that particular model. Thus, though rooted in relational technology, SQL looks set to supersede the world of relational databases and continue to be the ubiquitous database language.

Notwithstanding, SQL is currently used almost entirely in the relational context. The next section will look at the principles and uses of relational databases. Such knowledge is vital for a proper understanding of SQL. The next section will also introduce some example databases that will form the basis of case studies that will be referred to throughout the text.

▓ 1.2 Database tables

▓ 1.2.1 What is a relational table?

In a relational database, everything is stored in tables.

A table is a two-dimensional object with rows and columns. Here is a table representing the membership of the (fictional) East Burbage Lacrosse and Hockey Club:

```
MEMBERS
INIT        SURNAME       TELEPHONE_NO        TYPE
____        _____       _____        ____

G           Swanson       021—564—8796        Junior
F           Yeung         0987—3438           Senior
Z           Bandar        061—257—1000        Novice
C           Kent          345—2131            Senior
P           Green         689—2134            Senior
O           Sharif                            Junior
J           Beck          345—2131            Senior
```

There are some things to note about this table.

1. The table has a name (MEMBERS). In a relational database, every table must have a unique name.
2. Each column has a name (INIT, SURNAME, TELEPHONE_NO, TYPE). In a relational database, every column must have a name. Within each table, the column names must all be unique. However, the same column names may be used in other tables.
3. Along each row and under each column there is one – and one only – value, i.e. each member has only one name, one telephone number and one type of membership. We call this the 'atomicity' property. Each row / column intersection has one, and one only, atomic (non-divideable) value.

   It is permissible for a column to have a blank value, e.g. O Sharif does not have a telephone number. When a value has not been assigned to a given row / column atom, we say this has the value NULL.
4. Column values do not need to be unique. (Note how C Kent and J Beck have the same telephone number and how membership types are shared between different members.) However, each row must be in some way different to all other rows in the table.

5. The values under each column conform to some sort of data type. All values under NAME are strings of alphabetic characters. All values under TELEPHONE_NO are numeric strings. Values under TYPE are character strings of a seemingly restricted range ('Novice', 'Junior', 'Senior').

In a minimally relational system, all data must be stored in tables which have the above characteristics. It follows, therefore, that all relational databases require a facility for defining such tables. Amongst other things, SQL provides this facility.

▨ 1.2.2 Relational keys

In point 3 above, it was remarked that all rows in a relational table must in some way be unique. Using the MEMBERS table, if we were to add a new Junior member called O Sharif who wasn't on the phone, our table would now look like this:

```
MEMBERS
INIT        SURNAME      TELEPHONE_NO        TYPE
____        _____      _____        ____

G           Swanson      021—564-8796        Junior
F           Yeung        0987—3438           Senior
Z           Bandar       061—257-1000        Novice
C           Kent         345—2131            Senior
P           Green        689—2134            Senior
O           Sharif                           Junior
J           Beck         345—2131            Senior
O           Sharif                           Junior
```

We now have two identical rows. If we were to perform a database query on this table looking for information on member 'O Sharif', there would be no way in which we could specify which of these two members we were interested in. In order to differentiate between members who happen to have the same name, telephone number and type, we need to add an extra column such as a membership number which will be unique to each row. For example:

MEMBERS

NO	INIT	SURNAME	TELEPHONE_NO	TYPE
1	G	Swanson	021—564-8796	Junior
2	F	Yeung	0987—3478	Senior
3	Z	Bandar	061—257-1000	Novice
4	C	Kent	345—2131	Senior
5	P	Green	689—2134	Senior
6	O	Sharif		Junior
7	J	Beck	345—2131	Senior
8	O	Sharif		Junior

The NO column now uniquely identifies each row in the table. We call this column the primary key. In a relational system, every table must have a primary key. Furthermore, no row may have a NULL value for its primary key.

It is possible for primary keys to be a composite of columns within a table. Suppose we wished to know what days each of these members was available for a match. We could not add a column (e.g. 'AVAILABLE') with a set of days indicating a player's availability as this would contradict the 'atomicity' principal described above. Instead, we would have to set up an additional table with a row representing each day that a given member is available, looking something like this:

AVAILABLE

NO	DAY
1	Saturday
1	Sunday
2	Saturday
3	Sunday
4	Saturday
4	Sunday
5	Sunday
6	Sunday
7	Saturday
8	Saturday
8	Sunday

What this table tells us is that member NO 1 is available Saturday and Sunday, NO 2 is available Saturday only, NO 3 is available Sunday only and so on. In this table, the member NO values are not unique. Neither are the DAY values. However, each row is different to all other rows. This is because each member NO/DAY combination is unique. We have here a composite primary key consisting of member NO and DAY. When a primary key is composite, it must be complete for every row in the table. In this example, if we had a row with a missing NO value or a missing DAY value, then its meaning would be indistinct. Thus we have the rule that no column that participates in a primary key may take the value NULL.

A relational database language must have the facility to enforce primary keys. SQL has this facility.

A primary key is a special form of candidate key. A candidate key is any collection of values that is unique to each row in a table. For instance, most business organizations assign a unique company reference number to each one of their employees. Employees will usually have a government-assigned reference number for taxation and welfare purposes which will also be unique to each employee. In this situation, the database designer must select one of these reference numbers as the primary key. A relational table may only have one primary key. Other unique identifiers are referred to as alternate candidate keys.

Apart from primary keys, there is another type of very important key in relational databases. These are foreign keys.

Note how in the AVAILABLE table we use the member NO key from the MEMBERS table to identify player availability. We call this a foreign key. Informally, a foreign key is a column that uses primary key values from another table. Foreign keys are ubiquitous in relational databases. They are the main way in which relationships may be established between one table and another.

Take, for example, the (fictional) Lower Neasden Health and Beauty Clinic. This enterprise administers a range of cosmetic treatments to various clients. Each treatment is administered by a therapist. In a relational database, we would model the enterprise as follows.

First, we would have a table listing the treatments on offer:

```
TREATMENT
REFNO      DESCRIPTION              CHARGE
_____     _____         _____

LS1        Emergency Liposuction    125.00
HT1        Minor Hair Transplant    250.00
HT2        Major Hair Transplant    500.00
BO1        Body Deodorization       100.00
```

In this table, REFNO acts as the primary key. Next we have a table listing the therapists, with a column THNO to give an individual identification to each therapist:

```
THERAPISTS
THNO       NAME
_____     _____

1          Dr Gray
2          Dr Lang
3          Dr Crippen
```

Now we have a table to list our clients, with CLNO as the primary key:

```
CLIENTS
CLNO       NAME
_____     _____

1          JP Gettysburg
2          D Green
3          G Lightly
4          P Pan
```

In order to record the administration of various treatments to the various clients, we require a final table thus:

```
ADMINISTRATION
CLNO       REFNO       THNO
_____     _____      _____

4          HT2         2
2          BO1         3
4          LS1         3
```

This last table (ADMINISTRATION) is entirely composed of foreign keys.

The first row tells us that client 4 (P Pan) is receiving treatment HT2 (Major Hair Transplant) from therapist 2 (Dr Lang). The reader might wish to work out what information the other rows convey. Assuming that each administration entry represents a unique instance of a particular treatment being administered by a particular therapist to a particular client, but that therapists may administer and clients may receive any number of treatments, then the primary key for this table is a composite of the three foreign keys.

In SQL, we have the ability to define foreign keys.

In the next chapter we will examine how we can define and build simple tables of data such as the ones above using SQL.

▓ 1.3 A very brief overview of SQL

SQL was originally developed in the 1970s in the IBM research laboratories as a prototype relational database language. The first commercial version of SQL was marketed by the ORACLE Corporation in 1979. IBM's first SQL-based product (SQL/DS) appeared in 1981, followed by DB2 in 1983. There followed a rapid expansion in the number of SQL products available, with approximately a hundred being on the marketplace by 1990. SQL had by now become the *de facto* standard language for relational database systems.

Official standardization has been undertaken. The first SQL standard was published by ANSI in 1986 ('SQL/86'), with extensions in 1989 ('SQL/89'). A revised and expanded ANSI/ISO standard appeared in 1992 ('SQL/92', or sometimes, confusingly, referred to as 'SQL2'). The early standards in particular were little more than an effort to codify that which was already provided by most SQL vendors. Although this rather limited the scope of the language, it did at least provide a platform for conformance and inter-operability between products. SQL/92 does have some features that go beyond those which already existed in the marketplace and there are very few products that fully support this latest standard. Fortunately, SQL/92 extends rather than replaces the vast majority of what was published before and most of SQL/89 was retained. Just some relatively minor parts were deleted, and these parts do not appear in this book. Thus, apart from the last chapter that looks at possible future directions for the language, everything in this book conforms to SQL/92 and when the phrase 'Standard SQL' is used in this book, it is SQL/92 that is being referred to. Most of the examples of SQL code given in the first nine chapters will also work on products that fully support SQL/89, though the text will point out when this is not the case. Chapter 10, however, requires a full implementation of SQL/92, while Chapter 11 includes material that relates to the next standard ('SQL/3') as well as research-based proposals that take SQL away from the 'pure' relational world.

There are certain features that are described in the standards as 'implementation-specific'. In particular, the way that database dictionaries are organized, how users are associated together in a database, how tables are stored and how a system is accessed ('logged onto') are left to the individual vendor. None of these product-specific features are addressed in this book. Optimally, the reader should have access to a relational database in order to try out the examples and exercises in this book. The precise details of how you access and get to use the SQL in your system will almost certainly be unique to your given product. Once into SQL, as stated above, everything in this book, except the material in the last chapter, should work on any product that supports SQL/92.

SQL can be used in one of three modes: 'module', 'embedded' or 'direct'. This book is written with the implicit assumption that the reader will wish to use the language in 'direct' mode. This is where the user enters SQL statements, typically on a terminal or a personal computer, that interact directly with a database. This is certainly the best way to learn the language. The other modes require the user to invoke an application program which has within it pre-coded calls to SQL code segments. This SQL code may be in a separately developed subprogram ('module' mode) or be embedded within the application code ('embedded' mode). Chapter 9 is specifically on Embedded SQL as this is by far the most commonly used method of invoking SQL calls within an application program.

There are three main elements to SQL: the SQL data definition language (DDL), the SQL data manipulation language (DML) and the SQL data control language (DCL). The SQL DDL is used mainly for defining tables and integrity rules. The SQL DML is used for inserting, retrieving, updating and deleting data in tables. The SQL DCL is concerned with table access and security.

▓ Summary

1. SQL is the most widely used of all database languages. It is rooted in relational database technology.
2. In a relational database, data is stored in tables consisting of rows and columns. Each column/row intersection in a table contains exactly one value.
3. Each column in a relational table must have a data type to which all values under it must conform.
4. Each row in a relational table must be different to all other rows in that table. This is achieved by designating a column or a set of columns to be the primary key for that table.
5. All columns that comprise the primary key for a table must have a value assigned for every row on that table. Other columns may have an unassigned (NULL) value.
6. A column in one table may contain primary key values for another table. Such a column is a foreign key. This is the main mechanism by which relationships between different tables is established.
7. SQL provides facilities for defining and accessing relational tables.

▓ Exercise

1. Examine the following set of database tables:

PATRON

NO	NAME	ADDRESS
7	K Miller	Frodsham House
5	K Earnshaw	The Haven
6	J Warren	Lower Uppingham
9	C Jason	The Docks

SHOWS

REF	NAME	WEEKNO
5N	Nothing On	5
7H	Hair to Eternity	7
8S	Seeds of Wrath	8

TICKETS

REF	TYPE	CHARGE
5N	Stalls	5.50
5N	Circle	12.50
7H	Lower Stalls	3.50
7H	Stalls	5.50
7H	Circle	10.00
8S	Stalls	5.50
8S	Circle	5.50

RESERVATIONS

NO	REF	TYPE	AMOUNT
7	5N	Stalls	5
5	5N	Stalls	2
6	5N	Circle	3
7	8S	Circle	2
6	8S	Stalls	3

The above tables list the regular Patrons of the Bugston Operatic Club productions, the shows that are put on, the prices charged for each show according to the type of seat and reservations made for tickets by the patrons.

Identify:

(a) the primary key columns for each table;
(b) the foreign key columns in each table. State which table is being referenced by each foreign key identified.

For each patron, work out which shows they have reserved tickets for and how much each set of tickets is going to cost them.

2 Building databases

SQL is a command-driven language. Using a small set of powerful commands, a user can define, populate, alter and retrieve data from a relational table.

In this chapter, we will be examining the use of the CREATE TABLE command for defining a database table and the INSERT command for populating a database table with data.

The CREATE TABLE command is part of the SQL data definition language. INSERT is part of the SQL data manipulation language.

2.1 Defining database tables

2.1.1 Columns and data types

In order to define a database table, a user needs as a minimum to name the table, name its columns and to define the data type for each column.

The MEMBERS table in Chapter 1 originally had four columns: INIT, SURNAME, TELEPHONE_NO and TYPE. INIT, SURNAME and TYPE were strings of characters whereas TELEPHONE_NO was a number. In order to define this table, we would need to give the following command:

```
CREATE TABLE MEMBERS
     (INIT CHAR (3),
      SURNAME CHAR (20),
      TELEPHONE_NO INTEGER,
      TYPE CHAR (10) );
```

This shows the basic form of the CREATE TABLE command. On the top line, we declare the name of the table and then in brackets we declare each column. The command is terminated by the semicolon. We have placed each declaration on a separate line for ease of reading and editing. This is not a strict syntactic requirement, but it is good programming practice.

With each column, we have declared its data type. INTEGER indicates a column that will accept only numbers and CHAR indicates a column that will accept strings of characters. With the CHAR data type, we usually indicate a maximum length for character strings in that column.

Standard SQL also supports the data types NUMERIC, DECIMAL, SMALLINT, FLOAT, REAL and DOUBLE PRECISION. Users will find that the majority of relational database products will also provide data types such as DATE, TIME, MONEY, LONGINT and so on. They will also provide data types that are the direct equivalent of the standard SQL data types, such as NUMBER for NUMERIC.

With the NUMERIC and DECIMAL data types, it is possible to specify the decimal precision of the numbers that may be entered under that column. For instance, in the TREATMENT table in Chapter 1, we had three columns: REFNO, DESCRIPTION and CHARGE. The CHARGE column consisted of numeric data in a money format, with two figures after the decimal point. In a system that did not supply a predefined MONEY type, using standard SQL we would have to define this table as follows:

```
CREATE TABLE TREATMENT
     (REFNO CHAR (3),
      DESCRIPTION CHAR (30),
      CHARGE DECIMAL (7,2) );
```

Here we are saying that CHARGE is a numeric column that accepts numbers that are up to nine digits wide, with a maximum of two coming after the decimal point. This allows for input values up to 99999.99.

█ 2.1.2 Altering a table definition

The table definition for MEMBERS provided above would give us problems when entering data under the TELEPHONE_NO. The example data had telephone numbers typically in the form '021–783-6523'. However, most systems would interpret this as a calculation, not an integer, and would store the result of this calculation (–7294) as the telephone number of this member. What this column is, in fact, is a string of characters which must be stored in the literal form that they are supplied to the system. In order to render this column definition correct, we must alter it. SQL provides the ALTER TABLE command for modifying and adding column definitions to a table.

In this situation, we could issue the command:

```
ALTER TABLE MEMBERS
MODIFY (TELEPHONE_NO CHAR (12) );
```

In theory, any column can be MODIFYed once declared. However, in practice, most products place restrictions on the use of MODIFY. Some systems will not allow a numeric column to be redefined as character or vice versa. Others may allow it as long as there is no data currently in that column. There are probably no systems that would allow such a redefinition to take place on a column that actually contained data.

Such problems do not usually pertain to such a degree when simply widening a column to contain more data of the same type. Suppose, for instance, we discovered that the DESCRIPTIONs of TREATMENTs were frequently more than 30 characters long. We can allow more space for DESCRIPTIONs by saying:

```
ALTER TABLE TREATMENTS
MODIFY (DESCRIPTION CHAR (60) );
```

In most relational systems, this command would pose no problems. Most, however, would not allow the user to narrow the width of a column that actually contained some data. There are ways around this, which will be described in a later chapter.

NUMERIC and DECIMAL columns can usually be MODIFYed in order to hold larger values with more decimal points without any difficulty.

Similarly, it is usually possible to respecify an INTEGER column as a DECIMAL column with a given precision.

As well as MODIFYing column definitions, SQL provides the capability to add column definitions.

In our MEMBERS table, we are currently missing the NO column that uniquely identifies members. To add columns, we again use the ALTER TABLE command thus:

```
ALTER TABLE MEMBERS
ADD (NO INTEGER);
```

Columns can be added to a table at any time. The only restriction is that they must have a name that is different to all other columns in that table. Once ADDed, a column may then be MODIFYed. There is no facility for removing a column from a table.

▓ 2.1.3 Removing tables

A table can be removed from a database at any time using the DROP TABLE command. The commands:

```
DROP TABLE MEMBERS;
DROP TABLE TREATMENT;
```

will remove these tables completely from a system. Their column definitions will be erased along with any data entered under these columns. Having removed these tables, the user may then use these names for new tables.

▓ 2.1.4 Defining keys

In Chapter 1, we mentioned the importance of keys in relational theory. To recap, each table should have a primary key which is a column, or collection of columns, that uniquely identifies each row in that table. No column that participates in a primary key may take a NULL value. A foreign key is a column, or collection of columns, in a table that contains primary key values for another table.

In SQL, we use the PRIMARY KEY clause in the CREATE TABLE command to identify primary keys. For instance, the MEMBERS table should be defined as follows:

```
CREATE TABLE MEMBERS
      (NO NUMBER NOT NULL PRIMARY KEY,
      INIT CHAR (3),
      SURNAME CHAR (20),
      TELEPHONE_NO CHAR (12),
      TYPE CHAR (10) );
```

We have extended the definition of NO to include not only its data type but also two constraints: NOT NULL and PRIMARY KEY.

NOT NULL indicates that every row in this table must have a value for this column. We do not need to restrict our use of NOT NULL to key fields alone. Any column can be specified as NOT NULL. We must, however, as a minimum ensure that primary key columns have the NOT NULL characteristic. PRIMARY KEY indicates that every row in this table must have a value for this column that is different to that for all other rows.

We can add constraints to columns using the ALTER TABLE command. If this table exists in the system without these constraints, we can issue the command:

```
ALTER TABLE MEMBERS
MODIFY (NO NOT NULL PRIMARY KEY);
```

The PRIMARY KEY clause may alternatively be used as a declaration that comes after the column declarations. For instance, the TREATMENT table could be declared thus:

```
CREATE TABLE TREATMENT
      (REFNO CHAR (3) NOT NULL,
      DESCRIPTION CHAR (30),
      CHARGE DECIMAL (7,2),
      PRIMARY KEY (REFNO) );
```

This form of declaration is required when we have a composite key consisting of two or more columns.

In Chapter 1, we had an AVAILABLE table which consisted of two columns: NO (referring to Member NO) and DAY. These two columns together comprised the primary key for this table. To declare this, we need to issue the command:

```
CREATE TABLE AVAILABLE
      (NO NUMBER NOT NULL,
      DAY CHAR (8) NOT NULL,
      PRIMARY KEY (NO, DAY) );
```

In this particular table, there exists a foreign key, NO, which is used to make references to the MEMBERS table. We can declare a foreign key in one of two ways:

```
CREATE TABLE AVAILABLE
      (NO NUMBER NOT NULL REFERENCES MEMBERS,
      DAY CHAR (8) NOT NULL,
      PRIMARY KEY (NO, DAY) );
```

or:

```
CREATE TABLE AVAILABLE
      (NO NUMBER NOT NULL,
      DAY CHAR (8) NOT NULL,
      PRIMARY KEY (NO, DAY),
      FOREIGN KEY (NO) REFERENCES MEMBERS);
```

Whereas a table may have only one primary key, it may have a collection of foreign keys, each of which may in themselves be composite.

In Chapter 1, we had a table ADMINISTRATION, which had three columns: CLNO, REFNO and THNO. Together, these three columns comprised the primary key for the table. Each column in itself was a foreign key to another table (CLIENTS, TREATMENT and THERAPISTS respectively). We would declare this table thus:

```
CREATE TABLE ADMINISTRATION
      (CLNO INTEGER NOT NULL REFERENCES CLIENTS,
      REFNO CHAR (3) NOT NULL REFERENCES TREATMENT,
      THNO INTEGER NOT NULL REFERENCES THERAPISTS,
      PRIMARY KEY (CLNO, REFNO, THNO));
```

In most systems, this command would be rejected if we had not already declared the CLIENTS, TREATMENT and THERAPISTS table. In such a situation, the user could instead give the above command without the

REFERENCES clauses and then later add them using the ALTER TABLE command.

NOT NULL is an example of a column constraint. This means that when altering a table to take a NOT NULL constraint on a column, we need to specify the relevant column using a MODIFY clause. FOREIGN KEY and PRIMARY KEY are table constraints, meaning that we can use the ALTER TABLE command using the ADD clause to specify keys. Thus, if we wished to retrospectively enter foreign key constraints onto a table, we can do so using ALTER TABLE thus:

```
ALTER TABLE ADMINISTRATION
      ADD (FOREIGN KEY (CLNO) REFERENCES CLIENTS,
      FOREIGN KEY (THNO) REFERENCES THERAPISTS,
      FOREIGN KEY (REFNO) REFERENCES TREATMENT);
```

▓ 2.1.5 Indexes

In a relational database, the rows that comprise a table may be stored in a completely random sequence. For convenience, all of the data examples up to now have been in primary key order. This is not, however a requirement of the relational model. A system that required rows to be entered and stored in a particular sequence would, in fact, contradict relational theory and would not be genuinely relational.

The requirement that rows be randomly sequenced can give rise to performance problems with relational databases. For instance, if the database user wishes to find a particular row which will have a unique value under one of its columns, typically a retrieval based on primary key value, the system will have to examine every row in the database until it finds that value. Worse still is the situation where a very small set of rows will be yielded by a particular query. Suppose, for instance, a travel firm wanted to contact all customers who had entered their place of birth as the planet Mars. Typically, this would be a very small set of people amongst a very large database of clients. However, the entire database would have to be examined in order to find, possibly, no records at all. More sensibly, the firm might want find the details of a client with a particular telephone number. Telephone numbers are not necessarily unique. Therefore, the entire database would have to be examined in order to yield probably just one record.

Most relational systems will have internal procedures hidden from the user that improve (or 'optimize') their performance when servicing a query. In SQL, the user has the facility to improve database performance by the use of indexes.

A database index is, in essence, just like the index to a book. Words in the text of a book are arranged into sentences, with their sequencing bearing no relationship to their place in the alphabet. In contrast, the words in its index are in strict alphabetic sequence. Finding an individual word in a book can be very time-consuming unless it has an index containing a sorted list of words and the page numbers where each word occurs. In such a case, finding the presence of a particular word in a text can be performed very quickly. A database index is the direct equivalent. It consists of an ordered list of database values for a particular column. Alongside each value is a list of the row addresses where that value occurs.

For instance, we could index the MEMBERS table in Chapter 1 according to their membership type. The index would look, in logical terms, something like this:

```
MEMBER_TYPE INDEX
TYPE        ROW

Junior      1, 6, 8
Novice      3
Senior      2, 4, 5, 7
```

This records the fact that the first, sixth and eighth row in the MEMBERS table has the value 'Junior' for TYPE, and likewise for other values. This brings the following benefits:

- Due to the ordered nature of the index, values may be found far more quickly than by directly examining the database table.
- Once a value is found in the index, the system need not examine any further index records as index values are unique.
- If a value does not exist in a table, this can be quickly established by looking in the index.

Indexes are especially beneficial when retrieving small, or possibly empty, sets of records from a very large database. They are also of great benefit when a retrieval requires data to be sorted in a particular sequence. In the above example, if we wished to retrieve MEMBERS records in TYPE order, the system would simply need to go down the index and retrieve records in the sequence found in the index. Without an index, the system would have to perform a sort on the database table itself before performing the retrieval. On a large table, this can be very time-consuming, even with very powerful machines.

In SQL, the CREATE INDEX command enables the creation of indexes over already existing tables. We basically need to name the index, name the table and name the column over which the index is to be created. So the above index may be created thus:

```
CREATE INDEX MEMBER_TYPE
     ON MEMBERS (TYPE);
```

This creates a single column index in ascending order of values for the column TYPE. Each value may have more than one row address stored against it.

We can constrain an index to have only one row address entry against each value. We would do this in the case of primary key indexes. The primary key for members is NO. We should create an index thus:

```
CREATE UNIQUE INDEX MEMBER_NO
     ON MEMBERS (NO);
```

We can create unique indexes on any column that we wish, not just the primary key.

Indexes may also be created on composite sets of columns. Suppose, for instance, that we anticipated a frequent requirement in TYPE order, but then alphabetically by surname within each TYPE. In order to speed up such a query, we would create an index thus:

```
CREATE INDEX MEMBER_TYPE_NAME
     ON MEMBERS (TYPE, SURNAME);
```

Composite indexes are, of course, required for tables with composite primary keys. An index for the AVAILABLE table primary key would be declared thus:

```
CREATE UNIQUE INDEX AVAILABLE_PK
     ON AVAILABLE (NO, DAY);
```

By default, index values are stored in ascending sequence. However, the user can modify this. If we wished to retrieve information on availability with Sunday records coming before Saturday records, we would have declared the index thus:

```
CREATE UNIQUE INDEX AVAILABLE_PK
     ON AVAILABLE (NO, DAY DESC);
```

DESC indicates that values for the DAY column will be stored in descending sequence. It has no effect on the sequencing of the NO column which remains in ascending (ASC) order. The order of declarations of columns is important. The above declaration causes the index to be sequenced by NO, and then by DAY within each NO. If we wished to have the index ordered by descending DAY sequence, and then by ascending NO sequence within each day, we would have said:

```
CREATE UNIQUE INDEX AVAILABLE_PK
     ON AVAILABLE (DAY DESC, NO ASC);
```

Although indexes can be beneficial in terms of data retrieval, they should be created judiciously. Although smaller than data files, they do, all the same. take up space. A table which is indexed over the majority of its attributes could effectively take up twice as much disk space. More importantly, every time a value is entered or changed in a data file, not only will the actual data file containing the rows of data have to be changed, but also any indexes over the column holding that value will have to be altered. Thus, although indexes will, on average, speed up data retrieval, they will also slow down the speed at which data can be entered and altered. Therefore, indexes over columns that are highly volatile in their content should be avoided.

As a rule of thumb, the database creator should create indexes over the following:

- primary key columns;
- any other columns or column combinations that must have unique values (i.e. alternate candidate keys);
- any other columns or column combinations where the data contents are expected to be stable and where data retrieval of a sorted nature is anticipated
- any other columns or column combinations where the data contents are

expected to be stable and where data retrieval will typically yield small sets of records.

Indexes may be removed at any time using the DROP INDEX command, i.e. DROP INDEX MEMBER_TYPE_NAME;

When querying or altering a database, the use of indexes is transparent to the SQL user. If an index exists that effects a query or an update of a database, then the system will find it. The SQL user does not need to specify the use of an index once it has been created.

■ 2.2 Populating databases

Having created a table, we can now enter data by use of the INSERT command. In its most basic form, INSERT allows the creation of data for one row at a time. The first row for the MEMBERS table would be declared thus:

```
INSERT INTO MEMBERS
VALUES (1, 'G', 'Swanson', '021–564–8796', 'Junior');
```

This creates a row in the MEMBERS table assigning values to the columns as declared in the CREATE TABLE command for this table.

Note how we have enclosed any CHAR type values with quotation marks. Numeric columns do not – indeed must not – have this requirement.

INSERT does not require that values be entered in the strict sequence of the CREATE TABLE command. However, any deviation from this must be specified thus:

```
INSERT INTO MEMBERS (SURNAME, INIT, NO,
TELEPHONE_NO, TYPE)
VALUES ('Kent', 'C', 4, '345–3121', 'Senior');
```

This is useful when creating a row which has a NULL value for one or more columns. For instance, some of our members do not have a TELE-PHONE_NO. We would create such a row thus:

```
INSERT INTO MEMBERS (NO, INIT, SURNAME, TYPE)
VALUES (8, 'O', 'Sharif', 'Junior');
```

Note how we are not necessarily INSERTing members in primary key sequence. This is because, as stated in 2.1.5 above, rows must be viewed in a relational database as being stored in an entirely random manner.

When INSERTing rows into a table, the SQL language will check that all values will conform to the declared data type for each column. It will also check for any constraints declared such as NOT NULL and UNIQUE INDEX.

For instance, the command:

```
INSERT INTO MEMBERS (SURNAME, INIT, TYPE)
VALUES ('Benaud', 'R', 'Novice');
```

will fail as the user has failed to specify a value for NO, which has the NOT NULL constraint placed on it. Likewise, the command

```
INSERT INTO MEMBERS (SURNAME, INIT, TYPE, NO)
VALUES ('Benaud', 'R', 'Novice', 1);
```

will also fail because the value 1 already exists in the UNIQUE INDEX built over NO.

Composite UNIQUE INDEXes only require that the combination of column values is unique, not individual column values. Thus, the commands:

```
INSERT INTO AVAILABLE VALUES (1, 'Sunday');
INSERT INTO AVAILABLE VALUES (1, 'Saturday);
INSERT INTO AVAILABLE VALUES (1, 'Friday');
```

are all perfectly acceptable. However, the commands:

```
INSERT INTO AVAILABLE (NO) VALUES (1);
INSERT INTO AVAILABLE (DAY, NO) VALUES
('Saturday', 1);
```

would both be rejected. The first would fail as a result of attempting to create a row with a NULL value for a NOT NULL column (DAY). The second would fail as it would attempt to duplicate a value in a UNIQUE INDEX.

It is fair to say that the use of INSERT for creating rows of data is rather tedious, and the majority of SQL-based products do provide alternative forms-based products for creating data. However, in most of these environments, the form is simply a front-end which is converted 'behind the scenes' by the system into an SQL INSERT command. Thus, many database users fire off SQL commands without ever realizing it.

INSERT can also be used in a highly efficient manner for copying large amounts of data from one table to another. This other use of INSERT, which is extremely useful, will be covered in the next chapter.

Summary

1. The SQL CREATE TABLE command is used for the initial definition of database tables.
2. ALTER TABLE may be used for changing column definitions using the MODIFY clause. Columns and table constraints may be added using the ADD clause.
3. CREATE INDEX is used for building indexes over columns and combinations of columns. CREATE UNIQUE INDEX may be used for enforcing primary key constraints.
4. Tables and indexes may be removed from a database using DROP TABLE and DROP INDEX.
5. Rows are built using the SQL INSERT command.

Exercise

1. Use CREATE TABLE and INSERT to build the example database given at the end of Chapter 1.

Make sure that you have declared all of the primary and foreign keys. Enforce the primary key constraints by creating appropriate indexes.

3 | Elementary queries

■ 3.1 Retrieving data from a table

The SELECT command is used in SQL for all forms of data retrieval. As such, it is a very powerful and versatile command, and it has a number of subclauses and variations. It is, however, essentially a very simple command to use as all SELECT commands take the same basic form. Informally, we can regard all SELECT commands as being structured thus:

```
SELECT *** give a list of columns ***
FROM *** state the table[s] being used ***
[WHERE *** state any constraints on what is being
retrieved ***];
```

As stated in Chapter 1, relational databases store data in tables. When we query a relational database, what we get back is a table. The purpose of the SELECT command is to build a table using data derived from the tables in a relational database.

For this reason, the first line in a SELECT command is a list of columns. This line describes the columns that will appear in the result of our query. The FROM line states the table(s) that are required to service the query. There is optionally a WHERE line which places some sort of constraint on what is being retrieved. Realistically, the vast majority of SELECT commands include the WHERE clause.

Using the THERAPISTS table from CHAPTER 1, to retrieve a list of therapists and their numbers we would say:

```
SELECT thno, name
FROM therapists;
```

giving the result:

THNO	NAME
1	Dr Gray
2	Dr Lang
3	Dr Crippen

This is an unconstrained command, resulting in all the rows from the given table. It so happens that we have retrieved all of the columns from the given table. The same result would have been achieved by saying:

```
SELECT *
FROM therapists;
```

If we just wanted to find out the names of the therapists, we would say:

```
SELECT name
FROM therapists;
```

giving:

NAME
Dr Gray
Dr Lang
Dr Crippen

As stated above, the vast majority of SQL commands will have some form of constraint placed on them. Users will usually wish to retrieve data from rows with particular qualifying conditions. Suppose we wanted to find the therapist number for Dr Crippen. To discover this, we would say:

```
SELECT thno
FROM therapists
WHERE name = 'Dr Crippen';
```

giving:

```
THNO
────
3
```

Such queries could return a set of rows. For instance, the query:

```
SELECT no,type
FROM members
WHERE surname = 'Sharif';
```

would give the result

```
NO  TYPE
──  ────
6  Junior
8  Junior
```

We would get this result as we have two members with the surname 'Sharif', both of whom are of type 'Junior'. The two rows in this result clearly refer to two different members. However, had we said:

```
SELECT type
FROM members
WHERE surname = 'Sharif';
```

our result would have been:

```
TYPE
────

Junior
Junior
```

Tables generated from SELECT commands that have duplicate rows are quite legal. In fact, they can sometimes be quite useful. The above result tells us that there must be two Sharifs on the members' list, both with the same type of membership. Sometimes, we do not want to get duplicate rows. For instance, suppose we wished to arrange a hockey match on a weekday. We might want to check our AVAILABLE table to see if there was anyone able to play on a weekday. The query:

```
SELECT day
FROM available;
```

would give us

```
DAY
____

Saturday
Sunday
Saturday
Sunday
Saturday
Sunday
Sunday
Sunday
Saturday
Saturday
Sunday
```

This would not be very useful if we had 100 members with about 200 availability records. More useful would be the query:

```
SELECT distinct day
FROM available;
```

giving:

```
DAY
____

Saturday
Sunday
```

We used here the DISTINCT clause in our SELECT command. This requires all rows generated to be unique. Any duplicate rows in the result must be removed. The result of this query tells the user immediately that trying to arrange a weekday match would not be feasible.

The constraint examples so far have been based on a value being equal to some other value. The full range of comparison operators can be used. For instance:

```
SELECT refno, description
FROM treatment
WHERE charge > 200.00;
```

will give us:

REFNO	DESCRIPTION
HT1	Minor Hair Transplant
HT2	Major Hair Transplant

Conversely:

```
SELECT refno, description
FROM treatment
WHERE charge < 200.00;
```

will give us:

REFNO	DESCRIPTION
LS1	Emergency Liposuction
BO1	Body Deodorization

Constraints may be combined. Another way of finding out whether a weekday match is feasible would be:

```
SELECT no, day
FROM available
WHERE day <> 'Saturday'
      and day <> 'Sunday';
```

This would yield an empty set. This is because the use of the 'and' operator requires that a row must satisfy both of the given constraints in order to be retrieved. Most systems would respond with a message such as:

```
no rows selected
```

A more precise search of the members table on name values would use initials as well as surnames, for example:

```
SELECT no,type
FROM members
WHERE surname = 'Sharif'
and init = 'O';
```

The 'or' operator may also be used to combine conditions. This requires that a row must satisfy either of the given constraints in order to be retrieved. The command:

```
SELECT no, day
FROM available
WHERE day <> 'Saturday'
or day <> 'Sunday';
```

would return every row in the table. This is because it is true for every row that either the day is not Saturday or the day is not Sunday. A more sensible use of 'or' would be a query to find everyone who is a Senior type member or who has the name 'Sharif':

```
SELECT surname,init
FROM members
WHERE type = 'Senior'
or surname = 'Sharif';
```

giving:

SURNAME	INIT
Yeung	F
Kent	C
Green	P
Sharif	O
Beck	J
Sharif	O

'or' and 'and' may be combined in a query. If we wished to eliminate P Green from the output, we might say:

```
SELECT surname,init
FROM members
WHERE type = 'Senior'
or surname = 'Sharif'
and surname <> 'Green';
```

This would, however, return the same output. This is because 'and' has a higher precedence than 'or'. Thus the conditions 'surname = 'Sharif'' and 'surname <> 'Green'' become combined into a single condition 'surname = 'Sharif' and surname <> 'Green''. The command retrieves all rows for which this is true (i.e. the two rows with the surname 'Sharif') along with all rows with the type 'Senior', which will include the row for P Green. In order to enforce the desired order of evaluation, we can use brackets thus:

```
SELECT surname, init
FROM members
WHERE (type = 'Senior'
       or surname = 'Sharif')
       and surname <> 'Green';
```

giving:

SURNAME	INIT
Yeung	F
Kent	C
Beck	J
Sharif	O
Sharif	O

The same result would be achieved with:

```
SELECT surname, init
FROM members
WHERE type = 'Senior'
      or surname = 'Sharif'
      and (surname <> 'Green');
```

Either of these formulations forces the condition 'surname <> 'Green'' to be evaluated separately from the other conditions and requires that all rows in the answer must satisfy this condition.

If we wished to find out which patient was receiving a Major Hair Transplant (HT2) from Dr Lang (therapist 2), we would say:

```
SELECT clno
FROM administration
WHERE refno = 'HT2'
and thno = 2;
```

giving the result:

CLNO
4

There is a problem with this result in that it does not tell us the name of the client. This is stored in the CLIENTS table. To discover this, we need to establish a cross reference between the ADMINISTRATION table and the CLIENTS table. Also, we would not necessarily know the primary key values 'HT2' and 2 for treatment and therapist respectively. It would be more natural to query the database on non-key values. In order to do this, we would have to establish further cross-references to the TREATMENT and THERAPIST tables. The process of cross-referencing in order to build queries happens all of the time in a relational database and is the subject of the next section.

■ 3.2 Cross-referencing data

■ 3.2.1 Simple joins

Many of the queries that are executed in a relational system require data to be retrieved from two or more tables. For example, using our Health Clinic database, we might wish to add the names of clients to the output derived from listing the ADMINISTRATION table. We would do this by establishing a cross-reference between CLIENTS and ADMINISTRATION based on the foreign key CLNO in the ADMINISTRATION table thus:

```
SELECT clients.clno, name, refno, thno
FROM clients, administration
WHERE clients.clno = administration.clno;
```

giving:

CLNO	NAME	REFNO	THNO
2	D Green	BO1	3
4	P Pan	HT2	2
4	P Pan	LS1	3

What we have built here is a new table consisting of data derived from two tables. In relational terminology, we call this a 'join'. The join performed above is probably the most common form of table join where the foreign key in one table is used to retrieve data from another table. However, joins may be established between any two columns where the data types are compatible, i.e. comparisons based on matching numeric values, matching strings of characters and so on. There are many other types of join, examples of which will be given at various stages of the text. Nearly all complex SQL queries involve some form of join.

In the example given above, we start by listing the columns that will appear in the output. Note how we have qualified the column CLNO with CLIENTS.CLNO. This is because a column with this name appears in both tables on the FROM line. SQL requires this qualification, otherwise the command has the potential to be ambiguous.

In the WHERE clause, we specify the relationship between the two tables with the phrase 'clients.clno = administration.clno'. This constrains the output to contain only those rows where the CLIENTS CLNO and the ADMINISTRATION CLNO are the same. This is what is known as an 'equijoin', a join based on the equality of two values.

Suppose we had not placed this constraint and simply said:

```
SELECT clients.clno, name, refno, thno
FROM clients, administration;
```

The result would be:

CLNO	NAME	REFNO	THNO
1	JP Gettysburg	HT2	2
2	D Green	HT2	2
3	G Lightly	HT2	2
4	P Pan	HT2	2
1	JP Gettysburg	BO1	3
2	D Green	BO1	3
3	G Lightly	BO1	3
4	P Pan	BO1	3
1	JP Gettysburg	LS1	3
2	D Green	LS1	3
3	G Lightly	LS1	3
4	P Pan	LS1	3

Here, we have caused all rows in the CLIENTS table to be joined with all rows in the ADMINISTRATION table. Due to the smallness of the data set used, we have a small, but meaningless, result. The consequences in a large database would be much more serious.

Sometimes in SQL we perform a join operation to service a query that only displays data from a single table. For instance, suppose we wished to discover the names of all hockey and lacrosse players who were available for a match on Saturday. This would involve matching all member NO values in the AVAILABLE table for Saturday against their corresponding names in the MEMBERS table. The query would be expressed thus:

```
SELECT init, surname
FROM members, available
WHERE members.no = available.no
and day = 'Saturday';
```

giving the result:

INIT	SURNAME
G	Swanson
F	Yeung
C	Kent
J	Beck
O	Sharif

In this query, we join the MEMBERS table and the AVAILABLE table over the NO key. We constrain the result by adding the condition 'day = 'Saturday''. We then further constrain the result by listing only the INIT and SURNAME column on the SELECT line. This is still a join operation. We are simply not displaying all of the columns that the operation will yield. Note how we do not need to qualify the INIT and SURNAME columns as they do not appear in more than one of the indicated tables.

The examples above join just two tables. In SQL, any number of tables may be joined in a query. At present, our query on the Health Clinic simply yields the names of clients receiving treatment. More useful would be a list including the names of the therapists and descriptions of the treatments being administered. This involves joining four tables: CLIENTS, ADMIN-ISTRATION, THERAPISTS and TREATMENT. We will exclude the key fields from our result. We would write the query thus:

```
SELECT clients.name, description, therapists.name
FROM clients, administration, therapists, treatment
WHERE clients.clno = administration.clno
and   therapists.thno = administration.thno
and   treatment.refno = administration.refno;
```

giving:

NAME	DESCRIPTION	NAME
D Green	Body Deodorization	Dr Crippen
P Pan	Major Hair Transplant	Dr Lang
P Pan	Emergency Liposuction	Dr Crippen

This particular query lists all treatments administered by all therapists to all clients. However, it may be the case that we are only interested in treatments administered by Dr Crippen. We can easily constrain the query thus:

```
SELECT clients.name, description
FROM clients, administration, therapists, treatment
WHERE clients.clno = administration.clno
and    therapists.thno = administration.thno
and    treatment.refno = administration.refno
and    therapists.name = 'Dr Crippen';
```

giving

NAME	DESCRIPTION
D Green	Body Deodorization
P Pan	Emergency Liposuction

We have not included the therapist's name in the output as we already knew this when writing the query.

These multi-table join examples are based around one table(ADMINISTRA-TION) which happens to have a lot of foreign keys. Joins may also be performed that establish cross-references across a number of tables rather than between one table and a number of others. Suppose, for instance, we had an extra table in our Hockey Club indicating a match fee for each type of member thus:

FEES

TYPE	AMOUNT
Novice	1.00
Junior	1.50
Senior	2.50

This indicates that Novices pay a fee of 1.00 per match, Juniors 1.50 and Seniors 2.50. We had a query above which generated a list of players available on Saturday.

Suppose there was also a transport levy due according to the day a match was played:

```
LEVY
DAY              CHARGE
____             _____

Friday           2.00
Saturday         1.50
Sunday           1.50
```

If we wished to generate a list of names of players available on a Saturday, along with the fees due from them and the transport levy to be raised, we would say:

```
SELECT init, surname, amount, charge
FROM members, fees, available, levy
WHERE fees.type = members.type
and    members.no = available.no
and    available.day = levy.day
and    available.day = 'Saturday';
```

giving:

INIT	SURNAME	AMOUNT	CHARGE
G	Swanson	1.50	1.50
F	Yeung	2.50	1.50
C	Kent	2.50	1.50
J	Beck	2.50	1.50
O	Sharif	1.50	1.50

All of the above examples involve joins based around the equality of key fields. However, joins may be established around non-key values and also around inequality. If we wished to exclude any members from the list whose transport fee was greater than their match fee, we would say:

```
SELECT init, surname, amount, charge
FROM members, fees, available, levy
WHERE fees.type = members.type
and    members.no = available.no
and    available.day = levy.day
and    available.day = 'Saturday'
and    amount > charge;
```

giving:

INIT	SURNAME	AMOUNT	CHARGE
F	Yeung	2.50	1.50
C	Kent	2.50	1.50
J	Beck	2.50	1.50

Amount and charge are non-key columns. However, we can perform a join over them as they have compatible data types (both decimal numbers). Moreover, the join performed here is based on inequality, namely the fee amount being greater than the charge levy.

▨ 3.2.2 Nested queries

SQL allows SELECT commands to be nested within other SELECT commands. This enables cross-references to be established between tables by means other than joining.

In the section above, we issued a join type command to find the names of all players available on a Saturday. We could have issued instead a nested command thus:

```
SELECT init, surname
FROM members
WHERE no IN
      (SELECT no FROM available
       WHERE day = 'Saturday');
```

We have here a query within a query. The inner query yields a set of NO values. The outer query uses the IN operator to match NO values from the players table against NO values yielded by the inner query.

Nested queries can be used for join operations where the result does not use columns from all of the tables involved in the operation.

For instance, we had a query above that yielded the names of patients and their associated treatments by Dr Crippen. Using a nested query, we could say:

```
SELECT name, description
FROM clients, administration, treatment
WHERE clients.clno = administration.clno
      and administration.refno = treatment.refno
      and thno IN
      (SELECT thno FROM therapists
      WHERE name = 'Dr Crippen');
```

Note how we have not needed to qualify the name column in the outer command as it exists only in one of the tables in the FROM line for this command. We still have a join in the outer command as the result consists of columns from more than one table.

With the inner command, we have a query that will yield only one row. When this is the case, instead of the IN operator, we could test for equality, i.e.

```
SELECT name, description
FROM clients, administration, treatment
WHERE clients.clno = administration.clno
      and administration.refno = treatment.refno
      and thno =
      (SELECT thno FROM therapists
      WHERE name = 'Dr Crippen');
```

Equality tests should be used with great care with nested queries as the user must be sure that the inner query will yield a maximum set of one row. The above query would fail if there were more than one Dr Crippen in the THERAPISTS table.

Queries may be nested within nested queries. Suppose we just wanted the name of patients treated by Dr. Crippen. We could encode this as follows:

```
SELECT name
FROM clients
WHERE clno IN
       (SELECT clno FROM administration
       WHERE thno IN
               (SELECT thno FROM therapists
               WHERE name = 'Dr Crippen'));
```

There is no join at all in this command as the result consists of columns from one table only.

Joins can be used in nested queries. For instance, the command above could have been written as:

```
SELECT name
FROM clients
WHERE clno IN
       (SELECT clno FROM administration, therapists
       WHERE administration.thno = therapists.thno
               and name = 'Dr. Crippen');
```

Nested queries should not be regarded simply as alternative means of writing joins. Joins that display columns from all of the tables in a query cannot be sensibly written as nested queries. Nested queries can do things other than joins.

They are especially useful for existence tests. Suppose, for instance, we wished to find the names of clients currently receiving treatments. We can do this with either a join or a nested query thus:

```
SELECT name
FROM clients, administration
WHERE clients.clno = administration.clno;
```

```
SELECT name
FROM clients
WHERE clno IN
       (SELECT clno FROM administration);
```

However, the join would yield three rows thus:

```
NAME
----
D Green
P Pan
P Pan
```

whereas the nested query would give us two rows:

```
NAME
----
D Green
P Pan
```

This is because there are three rows in the ADMINISTRATION table that can satisfy the join condition, giving us three rows in the result. The nested query alternatively finds two rows in the Clients table whose CLNO is in the set of CLNO values returned by the nested query.

This difference between the behaviour of nested queries and joins is further illustrated if we reverse this query to try and discover the names of clients currently receiving no treatment. With the join written thus:

```
SELECT name
FROM clients, administration
WHERE clients.clno <> administration.clno;
```

we would get:

```
NAME
----
JP Gettysburg
D Green
G Lightly
JP Gettysburg
G Lightly
P Pan
JP Gettysburg
D Green
G Lightly
```

What the query does is to match client rows against every administration row that has a CLNO different to the client's CLNO. This tells us, for each treatment, the clients who do not receive that treatment. This answer is not what the user required. However, the nested query:

```
SELECT name
FROM clients
WHERE clno NOT IN
        (SELECT clno FROM administration);
```

would give us:

```
NAME
─────

JP Gettysburg
G Lightly
```

which equates to the right answer.

There are many other situations where nested queries are required to provide the right answer. These will be examined in later chapters.

■ 3.2.3 The nested INSERT

In the previous chapter, the use of INSERT for creating single rows of data was demonstrated. INSERT can also be used for creating rows of data that are copied from another table (or tables). This is done by nesting a SELECT command into the INSERT command.

Suppose, for instance, we had access to a database table of potential players for our Hockey and Lacrosse Club, which had the columns PLNO, PLNAME, TEL_NO that equated to and have the same data type as the NO, SURNAME and TELEPHONE_NO columns in our MEMBERS table. We could copy this data over thus:

```
INSERT INTO MEMBERS (NO, SURNAME, TELEPHONE_NO)
SELECT plno, plname, tel_no
FROM players;
```

The nested SELECT command may itself have a join, a further nested SELECT or a constraint. For instance, if we wished to debar any players with the name 'Earnshaw', we would say:

```
INSERT INTO MEMBERS (NO, SURNAME, TELEPHONE_NO)
SELECT plno, plname, tel_no
FROM players
WHERE plname <> 'Earnshaw';
```

When two tables have a completely compatible set of columns, we can do a straightforward copy thus:

```
INSERT INTO RETIRED_MEMBERS
SELECT * FROM MEMBERS;
```

This would copy the entire MEMBERS table into another table called RETIRED_MEMBERS. This would work as long as this other table had the same number of columns as the MEMBERS table, and the data type of each MEMBERS column was compatible with the corresponding column in the RETIRED_MEMBERS table. By corresponding, we mean the first column in one table corresponds to the first column in another table, the second column to the second and so on. It is the column positions that correspond. They may have different names.

A further constraint on the successful execution of inserts is the existence of primary keys and unique indexes. Each of the commands above would fail if, amongst the set of rows to be copied from one table to another, there existed in the relevant corresponding columns any values that represented a duplication of primary key values or any other column values specified as being unique in the target table. For instance, if there was any player whose PLNO value replicated a NO value that already existed in the MEMBERS table, then the entire INSERT command would fail.

A guard against this would be to extend the command thus:

```
INSERT INTO MEMBERS(NO, SURNAME, TELEPHONE_NO)
SELECT plno,plname,tele_no
FROM players
WHERE plno NOT IN
      (SELECT no FROM MEMBERS);
```

This might result in not all player rows being copied across. The user would also need to issue the command

```
SELECT * FROM PLAYERS
WHERE plno NOT IN
        (SELECT no FROM members);
```

to discover who, if anyone, had not been copied.

▓ 3.3 Altering data in tables

We have examined until now how to enter and retrieve data from tables. In a realistic database, we would also wish to change the content of tables by deleting and altering data.

▓ 3.3.1 Deleting rows

In SQL, the DELETE command removes rows from tables. It is used thus:

```
DELETE FROM *** table ***
WHERE *** rows meeting some condition ***;
```

For instance, if we wished to remove Dr Crippen from our database, we would say:

```
DELETE FROM therapists
WHERE name = 'Dr Crippen';
```

This command would remove the third row from the example table of Therapists.

The following command would remove two rows from the MEMBERS table:

```
DELETE FROM members
WHERE surname = 'Sharif';
```

This is because there are two rows that satisfy the given condition.

We might have decided to remove Dr Crippen from the database because he had the misfortune to have killed off all of his patients. Thus, before issuing the first DELETE command above, we could have said:

```
DELETE FROM clients
WHERE clno IN
        (SELECT clno FROM administration, therapists
         WHERE therapists.thno = administration.thno
         and name = 'Dr Crippen');
```

This would have the effect of removing all clients treated by Dr Crippen. The WHERE clause contains a nested SQL statement that yields the client numbers of all patients whose administration record has a therapist number that matches that of Dr Crippen. This is done by performing a conditional join of ADMINISTRATION and THERAPISTS. Any patient whose CLNO is in the resulting set is removed from the CLIENTS table.

The WHERE line is optional in the DELETE command. The following command has no WHERE clause and would thus have the effect of removing all data from the given table:

```
DELETE FROM clients;
```

The table would still, however, exist in the database. Complete removal would only be achieved by the DROP TABLE command.

▨ 3.3.2 Changing rows

The UPDATE command is used for changing data values in tables.

A simple UPDATE follows:

```
UPDATE members
SET surname = 'Hari'
WHERE no = 1;
```

This has the effect of changing the surname of member NO 1 from Swanson to Hari. This changes just one row as there is only one row that meets this condition. We can update a whole set of rows. For instance, if we wished to redesignate the Junior title to Colt, we would say:

```
UPDATE members
SET type = 'Colt'
WHERE type = 'Junior';
```

This would change all rows with the value 'Junior' for TYPE to 'Colt' as the TYPE value.

The WHERE clause is optional. We can change all the rows to have a particular column value by omitting this clause. For instance, the command:

```
UPDATE members
SET type = 'Senior';
```

would designate all members to have the TYPE value 'Senior'.

Sets of columns can be used in the UPDATE command. The following command would have the effect of setting all members with the name 'F Yeung' to Junior type membership with the telephone number 1234567:

```
UPDATE members
SET type = 'Junior', telephone_no = '1234567'
WHERE surname = 'Yeung'
      and init = 'F';
```

A further variant on the SET clause is to nest a SELECT command to extract values from the database. This command will cause all members with the name 'O Sharif' to have the same telephone number as Z Bandar:

```
UPDATE members
SET telephone_no = (SELECT telephone_no
                    FROM members
                    WHERE surname = 'Bandar'
                    and init = 'Z')
WHERE surname = 'Sharif'
      and init = 'O';
```

When using this variant of the UPDATE command, care must be taken to ensure that the nested query yields exactly one value.

Expressions may be used in the SET clause. The following command increases all fee amounts by 10%:

```
UPDATE fees
SET amount = amount * 1.1;
```

In the section above, we removed all patients from our clinic who had been treated by Dr Crippen. We may instead have added an extra column 'STATUS' and set this to 'Deceased' for all of his patients thus:

```
ALTER TABLE CLIENTS
ADD (STATUS CHAR (20) );
```

```
UPDATE CLIENTS
SET status = 'Deceased'
WHERE clno IN
        (SELECT clno FROM administration, therapists
        WHERE therapists.thno = administration.thno
        and name = 'Dr Crippen');
```

▓ Summary

1. The SQL SELECT command is used for all forms of data retrieval.
2. The SELECT command builds tables using data from one or more tables within a database.
3. Queries that require more than one table may be built using joins or nested queries.
4. Nested queries can be used with INSERT to build rows using data from other tables.
5. The DELETE command removes rows from tables.
6. The UPDATE command changes data in tables. It can make use of nested queries in order to copy data from other tables or within tables.

▓ Exercises

Using the example database that you built in Chapter 2:

1. Write queries to:
    (a) yield the names of all patrons;
    (b) yield the price of the different types of ticket for each show;
    (c) yield the reference nos of shows for which tickets have been booked. This list should not contain any duplicates;
    (d) Yield the names of all shows for which tickets have been booked. Write this query as a join and as a nested query;
    (e) Yield, for each booking made, the name of the patron, the name of the show, the type of the ticket, the cost of the ticket and the amount of tickets sold;
    (f) yield the names of shows for which no bookings have been made;
    (g) Yield the names of patrons who have made no bookings.
2. Use an INSERT command to copy all clients from the CLIENTS table into the PATRONS table.
3. Use UPDATE commands to enter addresses for each client copied above.

Having entered individual addresses, use UPDATE to copy D Green's address to P Pan's address.

4. Write DELETE commands to:
   (a) remove all patrons called 'D Green';
   (b) remove all patrons who have received an Emergency Liposuction;
   (c) remove all patrons who have been treated by Dr Crippen;
   (d) remove all patrons who have not booked any tickets for any shows.

4 Views

4.1 What is a view?

Up to this point in the text, we have been considering relational databases in terms of base tables only.

A base table is a representation of the data that is physically stored in a relational database. The data content of a relational database is the sum of all of its base tables. There is, however, another form of table in a relational database: a view.

A view is a table that is derived from one or more other tables. It can be thought of as a logical table rather than a physical table. For instance, with our MEMBERS table, there may be occasions where we only wish to deal with the subset that represents senior members only. Such a subset would be thus:

SENIORS

NO	INIT	SURNAME	TELEPHONE_NO	TYPE
2	F	Yeung	0987—3748	Senior
4	C	Kent	345—2131	Senior
5	P	Green	689—2134	Senior
7	J	Beck	345—2131	Senior

As with base tables, a view must have a unique name. As they are derived from other tables, they must have some sort of defining condition. This particular view is defined as all rows in the MEMBERS table with the TYPE value 'Senior'. Having defined our view, we can then refer to it as if it were another table. (There are restrictions in SQL as to what can be done with views which will be explained later.)

The view above has an element of redundancy. The TYPE column is hardly necessary as the defining condition constrains it to having the value 'Senior'. A view may also be a subset of columns. Thus, a more sensible view would be:

```
SENIORS
NO    INIT   SURNAME        TELEPHONE_NO
──    ────   ───────        ────────────
2     F      Yeung          0987—3748
4     C      Kent           345—2131
5     P      Green          689—2134
7     J      Beck           345—2131
```

Views may also be derived from more than one table. It would probably be convenient to have a table in our Health Clinic that matched the names of patients against their treatments and therapists thus:

```
CONSULTANCIES
CLIENT        TREATMENT                  THERAPIST
──────        ─────────                  ─────────
P Pan         Major Hair Transplant      Dr Lang
D Green       Body Deodorization         Dr Crippen
P Pan         Emergency Liposuction      Dr Crippen
```

This view is built over a join of the CLIENTS, TREATMENTS, THERAPISTS and ADMINISTRATION tables. From this join, we have only used the columns that are of interest to us: NAME from CLIENTS, DESCRIPTION from TREATMENTS and NAME from THERAPISTS. Furthermore, we have retitled these columns as CLIENT, TREATMENT and THERAPIST respectively. This retitling has no effect on the definition of the respective base tables. It has been done in order to render the output of the view more sensible by the use of meaningful column names. The retitling of base table columns in views is permissible and, in situations such as this, desirable.

Above it was stated that a view may be derived from one or more tables in a relational database. As a view is in itself a table, we may build views from existing views or a combination of views and base tables.

We may wish to have a view of Dr Crippens consultancies only. There are two ways in which this could be defined. One would be to write a join of the four base tables necessary to service this query. The other would be to derive a subset from the CONSULTANCIES view above. The second strategy would be a much easier process. The result would be the same:

```
CRIPPENS_CONSULTANCIES
CLIENT          TREATMENT
_____        _____

D Green         Body Deodorization
P Pan           Emergency Liposuction
```

Why do we have views in a relational database? Here are some reasons stated informally:

- **Convenience.** Views may be regarded as a form of shorthand for writing queries. In the SENIORS example above, the SQL query for retrieving this information using the base table would be:

  ```
  SELECT no, init, surname, telephone_no
  FROM members
  WHERE type = 'Senior';
  ```

  Using the view, we would say:

  ```
  SELECT * FROM Seniors;
  ```

  With a view built over a join, the saving in coding effort is even more dramatic. Thus, views provide a form of 'macro' capability for an SQL programmer.
- **Versatility.** A large database may have many different types of user, sharing the same data but making different uses of it. One representation of the database may appear logical and useful to one class of user but may be completely useless for another. By creating views, a database may be logically restructured in a variety of ways enabling different types of user to focus on those aspects that are of particular interest to them.
- **Security.** In a multi-user database system, it is frequently the case that you do not wish all users to have access to all of the data. One level of security restriction is to bar access to certain base tables to certain users.

However, this may be too crude a mechanism, resulting in some users being locked out from information that they legitimately require. Typically, they may require access to subsets of various tables. The view mechanism allows a database administrator to provide controlled access to subsets of data. By granting access through views, the administrator can effectively hide sections of the database from unauthorized users while still enabling them to have access to the data that they require.

* **Protection against restructuring.** It is in the nature of a long-term database that it will grow and occasionally be restructured. Columns may be added to tables. Base tables may be subdivided, either horizontally or vertically. (A horizontal subdivision would be to create tables based on subsets of rows from an existing table. A vertical subdivision would be to create new tables based on subsets of columns from an existing table. In each situation, the existing base table should then be destroyed otherwise the database will have an uneccessary and dangerous duplication of information.) This will have the effect of rendering obsolete the SQL queries that use such base tables. Rather than rewrite all these queries, it is far more convenient and productive to create views that logically recreate the previous structure of the database. By giving the views the same names as the previously existing tables, the SQL query code invoked by the database users can remain unaltered.

Views are thus an important and useful feature of relational databases. In SQL, we have the ability to define and use views.

▦ 4.2 Building views in SQL

In SQL, we use the CREATE VIEW command to define a view.

As stated above, a view is a table that derives its content from one or more tables in a relational database. In SQL, we derive a view by embedding a SELECT command within a CREATE VIEW command.

In the first example above, we had a view called SENIORS which was derived from the MEMBERS table, its defining condition being all members with the TYPE value 'Senior'. To define this in SQL, we would say:

```
CREATE VIEW Seniors
AS SELECT no, init, surname, telephone_no
   FROM members
   WHERE type = 'Senior';
```

In this example, the view SENIORS takes the columns NO, INIT, SURNAME and TELEPHONE_NO from the base table MEMBERS. Along with the column names, the view will inherit the respective data types of the given columns.

In our second example above, we had a view that was derived from a join of four base tables. The output was a table containing just three columns from these tables. Furthermore, they were retitled. We would define this view as follows:

```
CREATE VIEW CONSULTANCIES (CLIENT, TREATMENT,
THERAPIST)
AS
SELECT clients.name, treatment.description,
therapists.name
FROM clients, treatment, therapists, administration
WHERE clients.clno = administration.clno
and treatment.refno = administration.refno
and therapists.thno = administration.thno;
```

In this example, we have declared the column titles for the view on the CREATE VIEW line. These titles derive their data from the equivalent column positions in the first line of the defining SELECT command, i.e. CLIENT is derived from clients.name, TREATMENT from treatments.description and THERAPIST from therapists.name.

We could have declared column titles in the first of our CREATE VIEW commands above, but this is not necessary when the column titles are going to be the same as those in the tables that service the view.

Our third example of a view above was one that was derived from another view: all consultancies by Dr Crippen. The simplest and most elegant way to declare this would be:

```
CREATE VIEW Crippens_Consultancies
AS SELECT client, treatment
FROM consultancies
WHERE therapist = 'Dr Crippen';
```

We do not need to provide column titles as we are using the titles from the view used to service the new view. Furthermore, this demonstrates clearly how Crippens_Consultancies is merely a subset of Consultancies.

Views may be removed from a database with the DROP VIEW command, for example:

```
DROP VIEW CONSULTANCIES;
```

This simply removes the name and definition of this view from the database. It has no effect on any underlying base tables or views. It will, however, have the effect of rendering invalid any views that use this view in their definition.

▓ 4.3 Manipulating views in SQL

▓ 4.3.1 SELECT commands with views

Any valid SELECT command can be used on a view. For instance, to find the telephone number for the Senior member Kent, we could say:

```
SELECT telephone_no
FROM Seniors
WHERE surname = 'Kent';
```

giving:

```
TELEPHONE_NO
```

```
345-2131
```

We stated 'could say' because the same information could have been obtained by querying the base table MEMBERS. However, as stated in 4.1 above, some users may only have access, for security reasons, to a database through views and would only be able to execute SELECT statements on views.

The user should take care to use the view names of any re-titled columns. For instance, the command:

```
SELECT description
FROM consultancies;
```

would be rejected as DESCRIPTION does not exist as a column name in the CONSULTANCIES view. It has been retitled as TREATMENT. Thus, the command should read:

```
SELECT treatment
FROM consultancies;
```

giving

```
TREATMENT
```

```
Major Hair Transplant
Body Deodorization
Emergency Liposuction
```

Joins may be executed using views. Views may be joined with other views or with base tables. For instance, to find out how much each treatment is going to cost in the CONSULTANCIES view, we would join it with the TREATMENTS table:

```
SELECT treatment, charge
FROM consultancies, treatment
WHERE consultancies.treatment =
treatment.description;
```

giving:

TREATMENT	CHARGE
Major Hair Transplant	500.00
Body Deodorization	100.00
Emergency Liposuction	125.00

The above is a join based on non-key columns. We have matched the name of a treatment in the CONSULTANCIES view with its description in the TREATMENTS table. If we had two treatments with the same description, we would get a result with two rows indicating two different charges for that treatment. In order to remove the possibility for such ambiguities, views that are built over joins should usually contain any foreign key columns within their definition. Thus, a 'better' definition of CONSULTANCIES would have been:

```
CREATE VIEW CONSULTANCIES (CLNO, CLIENT, REFNO,
                           TREATMENT, THNO, THERAPIST)
AS
SELECT clients.clno, clients.name, treatment.refno,
       description, therapists.thno, therapists.name
```

```
FROM clients, treatment, therapists, administration
WHERE clients.clno = administration.clno
and treatment.refno = administration.refno
and therapists.thno = administration.thno;
```

We would then do the join example given above as:

```
SELECT treatment, charge
FROM consultancies, treatment
WHERE consultancies.refno = treatment.refno;
```

The join is now based on a foreign key, meaning that each row in the CONSULTANCIES view cannot be joined with more than one row in the TREATMENTS table, giving an unambiguous charge for each consultancy.

■ 4.3.2 UPDATE, DELETE and INSERT commands with views

Wheareas any valid SELECT command may be used with a view, in SQL there are restrictions placed on the use of UPDATE, DELETE and INSERT commands. These commands may only be used on views that derive their data, either directly or indirectly, from one base table. In the example views given in this chapter, SENIORS may have its contents altered by the use of these commands, whereas CONSULTANCIES and CRIPPENS_ CONSULTANCIES may not. This is because SENIORS is derived from the base table MEMBERS alone, whereas the other two are derived from a join of CLIENTS, TREATMENTS, ADMINISTRATION and THERAPISTS. Views that may have these commands executed on them are termed 'updateable'. A more precise definition of updateable views is given later in the text when we have presented some more advanced aspects of SQL.

A view that is derived from an updateable view may also be updateable. Thus a view such as:

```
CREATE VIEW TELENOS
AS SELECT no, telephone_no
FROM Seniors;
```

is updateable as it is derived from an updateable view.

However, the view:

```
CREATE VIEW TREATMENTS
AS select treatment, client
FROM consultancies;
```

would not be updateable as it is derived from a non-updateable view.

When a view is updateable, then the full syntax of INSERT, UPDATE and DELETE may be used on it. Care should be taken when using these commands on views as they directly affect the rows in the underlying base table. Conversely, any UPDATE, DELETE and INSERT commands on a base table will effect any views derived from that base table. For instance, the command:

```
DELETE FROM Seniors
WHERE surname = 'Kent';
```

will be translated by the system into:

```
DELETE FROM members
WHERE surname = 'Kent'
and type = 'Senior';
```

The last line of this command indicates the condition upon which the view SENIORS is derived.

The command:

```
UPDATE Seniors
SET name = 'Clapton'
WHERE name = 'Beck';
```

will cause the corresponding row in the MEMBERS table to have its name changed.

The command:

```
UPDATE members
SET type = 'Junior'
WHERE surname = 'Kent';
```

will have the effect of removing this row from the SENIORS as it no longer satisfies the defining condition.

In theory, rows may be inserted through an updateable view. However, the following command would be ambiguous semantically:

```
INSERT INTO Seniors
VALUES (12, 'A', 'Nother', '246—81012');
```

This command is syntactically correct and would have the effect of creating a new row in the MEMBERS base table with the given values for NO, INIT, SURNAME and TELEPHONE_NO. However, this row would not appear in any subsequent SELECT commands performed on the Seniors view. This is because the view is defined as being all members with the TYPE value 'Senior'. This particular row has a NULL entry for its TYPE value. It will therefore not appear in the view through which it was created. In order for this to happen, the subsequent command:

```
UPDATE MEMBERS
SET type = 'Senior'
WHERE no = 12;
```

will have to be given.

▓ Summary

1. In a relational database, there are two kinds of table: base tables and views.
2. A view is a logical table that is derived from a set of one or more base tables, either directly or indirectly.
3. Views are defined in SQL using a SELECT command indicating the conditions and tables that they are based upon.
4. SQL SELECT commands may be used on views in the same way as they are used on base tables.
5. SQL INSERT, UPDATE and DELETE commands may only be used on updateable views. A view is updateable when it is derived from a single base table or from an updateable view.

▓ Exercise

1. Using the example database from previous chapters, define a view that holds the names of patrons, the types of tickets they have booked and the shows that they have reserved each ticket type for. It should have the following column headings:

PATRON   SHOW TICKET_TYPE   QUANTITY

Is this view updateable? Give a reason for your answer.

Write a query using this view to show the name and address of each patron and the show(s) that they have booked tickets for.

What ambiguity could result from this query? How should it be resolved?

5 Processing data

In previous chapters, we have given examples of queries that retrieve and alter data held in tables. SQL also provides facilities for processing the data derived in a SELECT command. In this chapter, we shall examine how simple reports can be generated using these SQL facilities.

5.1 SQL expressions

In all of the SQL SELECT examples given in previous chapters, we retrieved a list of columns using a list of tables. Columns and tables are, in themselves, SQL expressions. An SQL expresssion can also take the form of a literal, a column expression, a psuedonym or a function. In this section, we shall examine column expressions and psuedonyms and give incidental examples of literals. Functions are considered in the next section.

5.1.1 Column expressions

A column expression may be defined informally as an operation using columns and/or literal values.

Numeric columns may be included in expressions using arithmetic operators. For instance, suppose that we wished to discover the effect of increasing the charges in the TREATMENT table by 10%. We could do this by retrieving the charge values and multiplying them by the literal value 1.1 thus:

```
SELECT description, charge*1.1
FROM treatment;
```

giving:

DESCRIPTION	CHARGE*1.1
Emergency Liposuction	137.50
Major Hair Transplant	550.00
Minor Hair Transplant	275.00
Body Deodorization	110.00

We have issued a command that increases the CHARGE values by 10%. This is for display purposes only. It this has no effect on the data in the underlying table. This can only be changed by the UPDATE command. Note how the literal ('*1.1') appears in the column heading.

The following operators can be used on numeric columns:

```
add:        +
subtract: -
multiply: *
divide:    /
```

Operations on numeric columns may combine columns with literal values or with other numeric columns. In our members database, we introduced tables indicating the transport levy for playing on a particular day and the match fee for different types of player. We discovered the cost to players playing on a Saturday using the following command:

```
SELECT init, surname, amount, charge
FROM members, fees, available, levy
WHERE fees.type = members.type
and members.no = available.no
and available.day = levy.day
and available.day = 'Saturday'
```

giving:

INIT	SURNAME	AMOUNT	CHARGE
G	Swanson	1.50	1.50
F	Yeung	2.50	1.50
C	Kent	2.50	1.50
J	Beck	2.50	1.50
O	Sharif	1.50	1.50

If we wished to discover the total cost to each player, we could include an extra column expression (AMOUNT+CHARGE):

```
SELECT init, surname, amount, charge, amount+charge
FROM members, fees, available, levy
WHERE fees.type = members.type
and members.no = available.no
and available.day = levy.day
and available.day = 'Saturday';
```

giving:

INIT	SURNAME	AMOUNT	CHARGE	AMOUNT+CHARGE
G	Swanson	1.50	1.50	3.00
F	Yeung	2.50	1.50	4.00
C	Kent	2.50	1.50	4.00
J	Beck	2.50	1.50	4.00
O	Sharif	1.50	1.50	3.00

Column expressions can be included in the WHERE clause. If we now wished to include only those players to whom the cost would be less than £4.00, we would say:

```
SELECT init, surname, amount, charge, amount+charge
FROM members, fees, available, levy
WHERE fees.type = members.type
and members.no = available.no
and available.day = levy.day
and available.day = 'Saturday'
and (amount+charge) < 4.00;
```

giving:

INIT	SURNAME	AMOUNT	CHARGE	AMOUNT+CHARGE
G	Swanson	1.50	1.50	3.00
O	Sharif	1.50	1.50	3.00

Character type columns may also be combined in expressions. Some versions of SQL allow the '+' operator to be used to concatenate strings. The SQL standard specifies the use of the '||' operator for this purpose. Thus, to concatenate initials and surnames in the above command, we would say:

```
SELECT init||surname, amount, charge, charge+amount
FROM members, fees, available, levy
WHERE fees.type = members.type
and members.no = available.no
and available.day = levy.day
and available.day = 'Saturday'
and (charge+amount) < 4.00;
```

giving:

INIT||SURNAME	AMOUNT	CHARGE	CHARGE+AMOUNT
GSwanson	1.50	1.50	3.00
OSharif	1.50	1.50	3.00

This particular command would benefit form the insertion of a period ('.') and space (' ') between the member's initial and surname. This can be achieved as follows:

```
SELECT init||'. '||surname, amount, charge,
amount+charge
FROM members, fees, available, levy
WHERE fees.type = members.type
and members.no = available.no
and available.day = levy.day
and available.day = 'Saturday'
and (amount+charge)  4.00;
```

giving:

INIT||'. '||SURNAME	AMOUNT	CHARGE	AMOUNT+CHARGE
G. Swanson	1.50	1.50	3.00
O. Sharif	1.50	1.50	3.00

Here we have combined two character type columns with a literal value ('. '). String type literals such as these must be enclosed in quotation marks. When a string type literal is specified in a column heading, it will then appear on every row of output under that column.

▓ 5.1.2 Psuedonyms

Column and table expressions may be assigned psuedonyms or 'aliases'. In the last of the examples given above, a more desrirable output would have involved the re-titling of those columns used in expressions. This can be achieved by use of the AS clause:

```
SELECT init||'. '||surname AS name,
       amount, charge, amount+charge AS cost
FROM members, fees, available, levy
WHERE fees.type = members.type
and member.no = available.no
and available.day = levy.day
and available.day = 'Saturday'
and (amount+charge) < 4.00;
```

giving:

NAME	AMOUNT	CHARGE	COST
G. Swanson	1.50	1.50	3.00
O. Sharif	1.50	1.50	3.00

Tables can also be renamed using an AS clause. The use of AS is optional, and is usually omitted. This facility can be very useful when writing join commands as above. By using aliases, we can save a lot of typing:

```
SELECT init||'. '||surname NAME,
       amount, charge, amount+charge COST
FROM members m, fees f, available a, levy l
WHERE f.type = m.type
and m.no = a.no
and a.day = l.day
and a.day = 'Saturday'
and (amount+charge) < 4.00;
```

In this example, we have specified an alias for each table on the FROM line, and then used these abbreviated aliases for our table references in the joins.

There are occasions when a query might wish to compare the contents of the rows in a table against rows in the same table. In this situation, the use of aliases is vital in order to remove ambiguities. For instance, suppose we wished to discover if there were any two members with the same telephone number. This would involve examining each row in the MEMBERS table and comparing its telephone number against all other rows in the MEMBERS table. We can achieve this as follows:

```
SELECT first.surname, first.init, second.surname,
       second.init, first.telephone_no
FROM members first, members second
WHERE first.telephone_no = second.telephone_no;
```

giving:

SURNAME	INIT	SURNAME	INIT	TELEPHONE_NO
Swanson	G	Swanson	G	021—564—8796
Yeung	F	Yeung	F	0987—3438
Bandar	Z	Bandar	Z	061—257—1000
Kent	C	Kent	C	345—2131
Kent	C	Beck	J	345—2131
Beck	J	Kent	C	345—2131
Beck	J	Beck	J	345—2131
Green	P	Green	P	689—2314

This command matches two tables against each other ('first' and 'second') which are both aliases for the MEMBERS table. The output tells us that Kent

and Beck both have the same telephone_number. However, it tells us this
twice as each table is matched against the other. Unfortunately, it also tells
us that every member has the same telephone_no as themself! We can remove
this redundant information by specifying that the MEMBER NO in First must
be less the the MEMBER NO in second. This removes all matching members
in either table who have the same NO, thus eliminating rows that tell us that
everyone has their own phone number. It also removes the duplication of
twice telling us that Kent and Beck have the same number (which a straight
test of NO inequality would not achieve). Thus the command:

```
SELECT first.surname, first.init, second.surname,
        second.init, first.telephone_no
FROM members first, members second
WHERE first.telephone_no = second.telephone_no
and first.no < second.no;
```

would give us:

SURNAME	INIT	SURNAME	INIT	TELEPHONE_NO
Kent	C	Beck	J	0345—2131

We can combine column aliases and literals to make this output much more
readable thus:

```
SELECT first.surname||' '||first.init||'.' NAME1,
       'has the same phone number as ' TEXT,
       second.surname||' '||second.init||'.' NAME2,
       first.telephone_no PHONE
FROM members first, members second
WHERE first.telephone_no = second.telephone_no and
first.no < second.no;
```

giving:

NAME1	TEXT	NAME2	PHONE
Kent C.	has the same phone number as	Beck J.	0345—2131

In this example, the literal 'has the same phone number as' has been
specified as a column expression, meaning that it will appear on every row
of the output.

▓ 5.2 SQL functions

▓ 5.2.1 Statistical functions

SQL has a number of built-in aggregate functions that can be used to provide statistical information derived from a table.

These are as follows:

```
COUNT:    returns the number of values in a column
          or the number of rows in a table;
MIN:      returns the lowest value in a column;
MAX:      returns the highest value in a column;
SUM:      returns the sum of values in a column;
AVG:      returns the mean of all values in a column.
```

For instance, to find how many members we have in the MEMBERS table, we would say:

```
SELECT COUNT(*) FROM members;
```

giving:

```
COUNT(*)
```
_____

8

The (*) with the COUNT function indicates that it is being used to count entire rows. COUNT can also be used on columns. To discover how many of our members had a telephone_no, we would say:

```
SELECT COUNT(telephone_no)
FROM members;
```

giving:

```
COUNT(TELEPHONE_NO)
```
_____

6

This counts the number of rows with a telephone_no value. It so happens that two of our members have the same telephone_no. If we wanted to find out how many different telephone numbers existed in the MEMBERS table, we would have to qualify the column reference with the DISTINCT function:

```
SELECT COUNT(DISTINCT telephone_no)
FROM members;
```

giving:

```
COUNT(DISTINCT TELEPHONE_NO)
_____

5
```

We can include more than one COUNT function call in a SELECT command. To find the number of members we have and the number of different types of member, we would say:

```
SELECT COUNT(*), COUNT(DISTINCT type)
FROM members;
```

giving:

```
COUNT(*)  COUNT(DISTINCT TYPE)
_____  _____

8         3
```

MIN and MAX can be used on both numeric and character type columns.

If we wished to discover the costs of the cheapest and the most expensive treatment in our clinic, we would say:

```
SELECT MIN(charge), MAX(charge)
FROM treatment;
```

giving:

```
MIN(CHARGE)     MAX(CHARGE)
_____     _____

100             500
```

As MIN and MAX both return only one value, they can be used to return a value from a nested query for comparison purposes. Suppose we wished to find out which of our clients were receiving the most expensive treatment. We would do this by joining CLIENTS, ADMINISTRATION and TREATMENT to yield patient/treatment information and then constrain this by only yielding those whose charge is equal to the highest charge thus:

```
SELECT name, description
FROM clients c, treatment t, administration a
where c.clno = a.clno
and t.refno = a.refno
and charge = (SELECT MAX(charge) FROM treatment);
```

giving:

NAME	DESCRIPTION
P Pan	Major Hair Transplant

MAX and MIN may also be used on character type columns. To find the member with the surname that would come first alphabetically, we would say:

```
SELECT MIN(surname)
FROM members;
```

giving:

MIN(SURNAME)
Bandar

It is illegal in SQL to mix column references and aggregate functions together in a SELECT command unless the command includes a GROUP BY clause (see next section). Suppose we wished to discover the full name and membership type of the member with the lowest surname. The command:

```
SELECT surname, init, type, MIN(surname)
FROM members;
```

would be rejected. MIN(surname) returns one value, whereas surname, init, type will return values for all rows in the table as there is no constraining WHERE clause. If we wished to find out more about this member, we would have to issue a nested query:

```
SELECT surname, init, type
FROM members
WHERE surname = (SELECT MIN(surname)
                 FROM members);
```

giving:

```
SURNAME    INIT  TYPE
_____   ____  ____

Bandar     Z     Novice
```

More than one type of function can be used in a command. If we wanted
to find out how many CLIENTS were receiving the cheapest treatment, we
would say:

```
SELECT COUNT(*), MIN(charge)
FROM clients c, treatment t, administration a
WHERE c.clno = a.clno
and    t.refno = a.refno
and    charge = (select MIN(charge) FROM treatment);
```

giving:

```
COUNT(*)  MIN(CHARGE)
_____  _____

1         100
```

The SUM function can be used on any numeric column. For instance, the
total cost of all treatments currently administered would be:

```
SELECT SUM(charge)
FROM treatment t, administration a
WHERE t.refno = a.refno;
```

giving:

```
SUM(CHARGE)
_____

725
```

AVG returns the arithmetic mean of a numeric column. Thus, the average
charge for all treatments would be:

```
SELECT AVG(charge)
FROM treament t, administration a
WHERE t.refno = a.refno;
```

giving:

```
AVG(CHARGE)
_____

241.67
```

A composite report giving the number of treatments administered, the highest and lowest charge, the sum of all charges and the average charge can be retrieved with one command:

```
SELECT COUNT(*), MAX(charge), MIN(charge),
    SUM(charge), AVG(charge)
FROM treaments t, administration a
WHERE t.refno = a.refno;
```

giving:

COUNT(*)	MAX (CHARGE)	MIN (CHARGE)	SUM (CHARGE)	AVG (CHARGE)
3	500	100	725	241.67

■ 5.2.2 Grouping statistical functions

The examples given in the previous section are all whole-table functions, that is they derive their result from performing the given function on all rows in a table. It is possible in SQL to perform a function on subsets of a table. This depends on the facility to define an expression by which rows may be grouped into subsets.

For instance, in our Health Clinic database, there are currently three treatments being administered to two clients. If we wanted to find out the sum of all charges on a client-by-client basis, we would have to group the clients according to that which differentiates them (their CLNO value). We achieve this as follows:

```
SELECT c.clno, SUM(charge)
FROM clients c, treatment t, administration a
WHERE c.clno = a.clno
      and a.refno = t.refno
      GROUP BY c.clno;
```

giving:

C.CLNO	SUM(CHARGE)
4	625
2	100

The above output indicates the sum of all charges for clients with the same CLNO value who satisfy the given join. When using scalar functions, it is only legal to SELECT column expressions that are included in a GROUP BY clause. Thus, the following command is illegal:

```
SELECT c.clno, name, SUM(charge)
FROM clients c, administration a, treatment t
WHERE c.clno = a.clno
      and t.refno = a.refno
      GROUP BY c.clno;
```

This is because there exists a column (name) in the heading that is not included in the GROUP BY clause. However, the following command would be quite legal:

```
SELECT c.clno, name, SUM(charge)
FROM clients c, administration a, treatment t
WHERE c.clno = a.clno
      and t.refno = a.refno
      GROUP BY c.clno, name;
```

giving:

CLNO	NAME	SUM(CHARGE)
4	P Pan	625
2	D Green	100

This is because we have now included name in the GROUP BY clause, meaning that the system will now process and return subsets of rows with the same combination of clno and name values.

As in the examples in the previous section, more than one function can be called in a SELECT command using a GROUP BY clause. For instance, the sum of all treatment charges, the average cost of each treatment and the number of treatments given to each client would be:

```
SELECT c.clno, name, SUM(charge), AVG(charge),
COUNT(*)
FROM treatment t, administration a, clients c
WHERE t.refno = a.refno
      and c.clno = a.clno
      GROUP BY c.clno, name;
```

giving:

CLNO	NAME	SUM(CHARGE)	AVG(CHARGE)	COUNT(*)
4	P Pan	625	312.5	2
2	D Green	100	100	1

This depth of analysis is not very meaningful for clients currently receiving only one treatment. It would be useful to constrain this to only those who have received more than one treatment. We can constrain GROUP BY clauses by the use of HAVING thus:

```
SELECT c.clno, name, SUM(charge), SUM(charge),
COUNT(*)
FROM treatment t, administration a, clients c
WHERE t.refno = a.refno
      and c.clno = a.clno
      GROUP BY c.clno, name
      HAVING COUNT(*) > 1;
```

This would now return just the first row from the previous result. HAVING tests each subset returned by the GROUP BY clause with a function value. In this case, the COUNT(*) function is applied to each subset and the result compared against the value 1. All subsets of rows which cannot satisfy the condition expressed in the HAVING clause (COUNT(*) > 1) are eliminated from the output. If we wished to retrieve only those clients whose average charges were greater than the average charge for all treaments currently being administered, we would say:

```
SELECT c.clno, name, SUM(charge), AVG(charge),
COUNT(*)
FROM treatment t, administration a, clients c
WHERE t.refno = a.refno
      and c.clno = a.clno
      GROUP BY c.clno, name
      HAVING AVG(charge) > (SELECT AVG(charge)
                  FROM treatment x, administration y
                  WHERE x.refno = y.refno);
```

giving:

CLNO	NAME	SUM (CHARGE)	AVG (CHARGE)	COUNT(*)
4	P Pan	625	312.5	2

This row is returned because the AVG(CHARGE) value of £312.5 for P Pan's treatments is greater than the average for all treatments currently administered (£241.67).

A client whose most expensive treatment was less than the average for all treatments currently administered would be:

```
SELECT c.clno, name, SUM(charge), AVG(charge),
COUNT(*)
FROM treatment t, administration a, clients c
WHERE t.refno = a.refno
      and c.clno = a.clno
      GROUP BY c.clno, name
      HAVING MAX(charge) < (SELECT AVG(charge)
      FROM treatment x, administration y
      WHERE x.refno = y.refno);
```

giving:

CLNO	NAME	SUM (CHARGE)	AVG (CHARGE)	COUNT(*)
2	D Green	100	100	1

In the last two examples, we have used a function call in a nested command to return a value for comparison purposes.

▓ 5.3 Ordering data

SQL provides the ORDER BY clause to enable the programmer to determine the sequence in which rows are retrieved by a SELECT command. By default, rows are displayed in the order that they are stored. Our MEMBERS table has been stored in primary key sequence. If we wished to display it in sequence of members' surnames, we would say:

```
SELECT surname, init, type
FROM members
ORDER BY surname;
```

giving:

SURNAME	INIT	TYPE
Bandar	Z	Novice
Beck	J	Senior
Green	P	Senior
Kent	C	Senior
Sharif	O	Junior
Sharif	O	Junior
Swanson	G	Junior
Yeung	F	Senior

Suppose that the second of our two members called Sharif changed their initial to 'B'. They would still be displayed in the sequence of rows returned by the SELECT command above. This is because the command orders the data by the surname alone. Beyond this, the data is retrieved in stored order. To enforce a more alphabetically correct sequencing, we should say:

```
SELECT surname, init, type
FROM members
ORDER BY surname, init;
```

Here we have specified a secondary sort key: INIT. This means that rows are first sorted by surname and then by init for matching surname values. If we wished to group together members of the same type, and then alphabetically within that type, we would say:

```
SELECT surname, init, type
FROM members
ORDER BY type, surname, init;
```

giving:

SURNAME	INIT	TYPE
Sharif	B	Junior
Sharif	O	Junior
Swanson	G	Junior
Bandar	Z	Novice

```
Beck      J      Senior
Kent      C      Senior
Green     P      Senior
Yeung     F      Senior
```

When sorting on a number of keys, it may be more convenient to refer to them by their position within the output rather than by name. The same effect as the last commannd can be achieved by saying:

```
SELECT surname, init, type
FROM members
ORDER BY 3,1,2;
```

This tells the system to sort by column 3 (type), then by column 1 (surname) and then by column 2 (init).

Ordering can be done on any column specified in a SELECT command. To retrieve client data starting with the client with the lowest total charges, we would say:

```
SELECT c.clno, name, SUM(charge)
FROM clients a, administration a, treatment t
WHERE t.refno = a.refno
      and c.clno = a.clno
      group by c.clno, name
      order by SUM(charge);
```

giving:

CLNO	NAME	SUM(CHARGE)
2	D Green	100
4	P Pan	625

All of the examples above give the output in ascending sequence order, which is the default for the ORDER BY clause. We can change this to descending sequence thus:

```
SELECT c.clno, name, SUM(charge)
FROM clients a, administration a, t
WHERE t.refno = a.refno
      and c.clno = a.clno
      group by c.clno, name
      order by SUM(charge) DESC;
```

giving the same output as before, but in a reversed sequence with P Pan's details at the top.

▧ Summary

1. SQL SELECT commands may use column expressions and table expressions.
2. Column expressions may include literal values.
3. Numeric columns may be combined into expressions using arithmetic operators.
4. Alphanumeric columns may be concatenated using the '| |' operator.
5. Tables and columns may be assigned psuedonyms.
6. SQL provides functions (COUNT, MAX, MIN, SUM, AVG) for returning values from a table.
7. Functions may return values from table subsets using the GROUP BY and HAVING clauses.
8. Output may be sequenced using the ORDER BY clause.

▧ Exercises

Using the Bogsworth Opera Group database:

1. Write the command to produce a report with the following headings:

```
PATRON_NAME   TEXT1   NO   TEXT2   SHOW   TYPE   COST
```

The patron_name column is the combined surname and initials for each patron who has bought a ticket for a show. TEXT1 consists of the literal value 'has bought'. NO indicates the number of tickets they have bought for each show. TEXT2 consists of the literal value 'tickets for'. SHOW is the name of each show they have bought tickets for. TYPE is the type of ticket. COST is the cost of each set of tickets bought. (Multiply the number bought by the cost of the type.)

2. Write commands to:
   (a) Return the total number of all tickets sold;
   (b) return the total sales revenue from all tickets currently sold;
   (c) return the total number of tickets sold for each production;
   (d) return the number of tickets sold and total sales revenue for each production (do this with one command);

(e) take the answer for (c) and subdivide this according to the type of ticket sold i.e. circle, upper stalls, lower stalls.

(f) take the output for (c) and constrain this to only those shows where the average price of each ticket sold is less than the average ticket price for all shows.

3. (a) Amend your answer to exercise 1 so that the output is returned in patron name order.

(b) Further amend this to return the output in show order, and then by patron name for each show.

(c) Amend your answer for exercise 2(c) so that the output starts with the show that has sold the most tickets and is sequenced downwards to the show that has sold the least. For any two shows that have sold the same number of tickets, sequence them downwards by the total cost of tickets sold.

6 Combining queries

■ 6.1 SET operators

Every SQL SELECT command returns a table. A table is, in itself, a set of rows. In SQL, we can use set operators to combine one set of rows with another. Suppose we had two queries which returned the following sets of rows:

```
Query A        Query B
A              A
B              B
C              X
D              Y
E              Z
```

SQL provides the UNION, INTERSECT and EXCEPT operators to combine these query results. The effects of these operations are as follows:

```
A UNION B:      Returns all rows that are in either
                or both sets:
                { A,B,C,D,E,X,Y,Z }
A INTERSECT B:  Returns only those rows that are in
                both sets:
                { A,B }
A EXCEPT B:     Returns those rows that are in SET A,
                but not SET B:   { C,D,E }
```

The EXCEPT operator is the equivalent of the DIFFERENCE operation from mathematical set theory. The above examples use two sets only. Multiple sets of data may be combined in complex expressions using more than one of the above operators. In order to do this successfully, the programmer needs to have a thorough understanding of set arithmetic. In this text, such knowledge is not assumed and we will keep to simple examples only. One thing to note is that the result of all of these operations returns a set without duplicates. Thus, in the first example, rows A and B only appear once in the result even though they exist in both query sets.

To use these operators in SQL, we require the following:

- two or more SQL queries;
- each query to return the same number of columns;
- each column in each query to be compatible with the equivalent column in the other query(ies). By this we mean that if the first column in the first query is of data type char, then all of the first columns in all of the other queries must also be of data type char, and so on.

▩ 6.1.1 The UNION operator

UNION merges the rows resulting from two or more SELECTs.

Suppose we wished to generate a list of MEMBERS of types 'Junior' and 'Novice'. We could discover this as follows:

```
SELECT no, surname, init
FROM members
WHERE type = 'Junior'
UNION
SELECT no, surname, init
FROM members
WHERE type = 'Novice';
```

giving:

NO	SURNAME	INIT
1	Swanson	G
3	Bandar	Z
6	Sharif	O
8	Sharif	O

As stated above, the UNION operator removes all duplicates from the result. Suppose we wished to generate a list of all members available on either Saturday or Sunday. We can achieve this as follows:

```
SELECT no, surname, init
FROM members
WHERE no IN (SELECT no FROM available
            WHERE day = 'Saturday')
UNION
SELECT no, surname, init
FROM members
WHERE no IN (SELECT no FROM available
            WHERE day = 'Sunday');
```

giving:

```
NO   SURNAME      INIT
---  ---------    ----
1    Swanson      G
2    Yeung        F
3    Bandar       Z
4    Kent         C
5    Green        P
6    Sharif       O
7    Beck         J
8    Sharif       O
```

Although a number of these members are available on both days, they each appear in the result just once due to the removal of duplicates from the result. Note how the primary key (NO) was specified in both commands. This is because the following command:

```
SELECT surname, init
FROM members
WHERE no IN (SELECT no FROM available
            WHERE day = 'Saturday')
UNION
SELECT surname, init
FROM members
WHERE no IN (SELECT no FROM available
            WHERE day = 'Sunday');
```

would give:

```
SURNAME    INIT
_____  ____

Swanson    G
Yeung      F
Bandar     Z
Kent       C
Green      P
Sharif     O
Beck       J
```

The second member called 'Sharif O' becomes lost. This is because there is nothing to distinguish this member from the other 'Sharif O' in the result. This can be overcome by use of the ALL clause:

```
SELECT surname, init
FROM members
WHERE no IN (SELECT no FROM available
            WHERE day = 'Saturday')
UNION ALL
SELECT surname, init
FROM members
WHERE no IN (SELECT no FROM available
            WHERE day = 'Sunday');
```

giving:

```
SURNAME    INIT
_____  ____

Swanson    G
Yeung      F
Kent       C
Beck       J
Sharif     O
Swanson    G
Bandar     Z
Kent       C
Green      P
Sharif     O
Sharif     O
```

The ALL clause allows rows to be duplicated. The effect here is to produce a list of all Saturday players followed by all Sunday players.

The above examples are all combinations of the same command using slightly different conditions. The first two could be implemented using the OR operator in a single command, for example:

```
SELECT no, surname, init
FROM members
WHERE type = 'Junior'
OR    type = 'Novice';

SELECT no, surname, init
FROM members
WHERE no IN (SELECT no FROM available
            WHERE day = 'Saturday')
         OR no IN (SELECT no FROM available
                   WHERE day = 'Sunday');
```

These would achieve exactly the same result as the first two UNION commands give above. However, the command:

```
SELECT surname, init
FROM members
WHERE no IN (SELECT no FROM available
            WHERE day = 'Saturday')
         OR no IN (SELECT no FROM available
                   WHERE day = 'Sunday');
```

would give:

SURNAME	INIT
Swanson	G
Yeung	F
Bandar	Z
Kent	C
Green	P
Sharif	O
Beck	J
Sharif	O

This is because the logic of the OR operator requires that a row is returned once it satisfies any of the given conditions. If it satisfies both the given conditions it will not be returned twice. Thus, OR does not have the same effect as UNION ALL.

The OR operator cannot be used to replicate UNIONs over different tables. For instance, a merged list of all THERAPISTS and all CLIENTS at the clinic can be achieved by:

```
SELECT name FROM therapists
UNION
SELECT name FROM clients;
```

giving:

```
NAME
_____

Dr Gray
Dr Lang
Dr Crippen
JP Gettysburg
G Lightly
D Green
P Pan
```

Furthermore, we can combine tables using completely different selection criteria. Here is a command to give the names of all therapists giving more than one treatment along with all clients not receiving any treatments:

```
SELECT name FROM therapists t
WHERE 1 < (SELECT COUNT(*) FROM administration a
            WHERE a.thno = t.thno)
UNION
SELECT name FROM clients
WHERE clno NOT IN
            (SELECT clno FROM administration);
```

giving:

```
NAME
_____

Dr Crippen
JP Gettysburg
G Lightly
```

▨ 6.1.2 The INTERSECT operator

INTERSECT returns only those rows that are returned by all of the given SELECT commands in a combination. Thus, the command:

```
SELECT no, surname, init
FROM members
WHERE no IN (SELECT no FROM available
          WHERE day = 'Saturday')
INTERSECT
SELECT no, surname, init
FROM members
WHERE no IN (SELECT no FROM available
          WHERE day = 'Sunday');
```

would give

NO	SURNAME	INIT
1	Swanson	G
4	Kent	C
8	Sharif	O

This returns those rows present in both sets of data, i.e. those members available on both the given days.

The AND operator is to INTERSECT what OR is to UNION. Thus, the above result would also be obtained using:

```
SELECT no, surname, init
FROM members
WHERE no IN (SELECT no FROM available
          WHERE day = 'Saturday')
AND   no IN (SELECT no FROM available
          WHERE day = 'Sunday');
```

As with OR, AND cannot be used to retrieve the intersection of two commands using separate tables, for example:

```
SELECT name FROM clients
INTERSECT
SELECT name FROM therapists;
```

It so happens that the above command would yield no rows from our example database. However, if there were any clients and therapists with the same name, it would reveal such a fact.

As with UNION, INTERSECT removes duplicates from the result unless INTERSECT ALL is specified.

▨ 6.1.3 The EXCEPT operator

EXCEPT returns all rows that are in one select command but not the next. Unlike UNION and INTERSECT, EXCEPT is not commutative. An operator is said to be commutative when the same result is achieved regardless of the order in which the operands are given. Thus, A UNION B will give the same result as B UNION A and A INTERSECT B will give the same result as B INTERSECT A.

(NB: Some SQL products use the word MINUS rather than EXCEPT.)

In all of the examples above, we would have obtained the same set of rows regardless of the order of the SELECT commands given (though the sequencing of the sets may have differed). However,

```
SELECT no, surname, init
FROM members
WHERE no IN (SELECT no FROM available
          WHERE day = 'Saturday')
EXCEPT
SELECT no, surname, init
FROM members
WHERE no IN (SELECT no FROM available
          WHERE day = 'Sunday');
```

would give:

NO	SURNAME	INIT
2	Yeung	F
7	Beck	J

whereas:

```
SELECT no, surname, init
FROM members
WHERE no IN (SELECT no FROM available
             WHERE day = 'Sunday')
EXCEPT
SELECT no, surname, init
FROM members
WHERE no IN (SELECT no FROM available
             WHERE day = 'Saturday');
```

would give:

NO	SURNAME	INIT
3	Bandar	Z
5	Green	P
8	Sharif	O

This is because the first command gives those who are available on Saturday only whereas the second one gives those who are available on Sunday only.

The command:

```
SELECT name FROM clients
EXCEPT
SELECT name FROM therapists;
```

would give the names of all CLIENTS who are not therapists, whereas:

```
SELECT name FROM therapists
EXCEPT
SELECT name FROM clients;
```

would give the names of all therapists who are not clients.

EXCEPT can always be replicated by use of NOT IN and a nested query, for example:

```
SELECT name FROM therapists
WHERE name NOT IN (SELECT name FROM clients);
```

▦ 6.1.4 Ordering combined commands

The ORDER BY clause can be used with commands combined around a set operator. Column names may differ between tables combined around a set operator. The ORDER BY clause must therefore use column reference numbers rather than literal column names. The clause may only appear at the end of the combined query thus:

```
SELECT surname, init
FROM members
WHERE no IN (SELECT no FROM available
            WHERE day = 'Saturday')
UNION
SELECT surname, init
FROM members
WHERE no IN (SELECT no FROM available
            WHERE day = 'Sunday')
ORDER BY 1,2;
```

giving:

SURNAME	INIT
Bandar	Z
Beck	J
Green	P
Kent	C
Sharif	O
Swanson	G
Yeung	F

The following:

```
SELECT surname, init
FROM members
WHERE no IN (SELECT no FROM available
            WHERE day = 'Saturday')
ORDER BY surname, init
UNION
SELECT surname, init
FROM members
WHERE no IN (SELECT no FROM available
            WHERE day = 'Sunday');
```

would be rejected.

▧ Summary

1. The results of SQL commands may be combined using set operators.
2. Two or more SQL commands may be combined as long as they are all compatible.
3. The set operators provided are UNION, INTERSECT and EXCEPT.
4. Duplicate rows may be returned by a set operator when used with the ALL clause.
5. An ORDER BY clause may appear as the last command of a set of combined commands.

▧ Exercises

Using the database at the end of Chapter 1:

1. Generate a list of Patron NO values for those who have made reservations for either 'Seeds of Wrath' or 'Nothing On'.
   Use a set operator to achieve this.
2. Extend the command above so that anyone who is attending both shows has their NO displayed twice.
3. Extend this into a nested command so that their names are displayed in alphabetic order.
4. Using a set operator and a nested command, write a command to show the names of patrons who are attending both of these shows.
5. Using a set operator, write a command to display names of patrons who are attending 'Nothing On' but who are not attending 'Seeds of Wrath'.
6. Write a command using a set operator to list any patrons who are not attending any shows.

7 Further types of query

7.1 The ALL and ANY operators

In Chapter 3, we introduced the IN operator that compared a value against a set of values returned by a subquery. We can also test against sets of values using ALL and ANY.

The ALL operator tests a given value against a set of values using a comparator ('equal to', 'less than', etc.). It returns 'true' if that comparator holds for all members of the set. For instance, given the numeric value 100, we can test this using the '<' operator against the following sets of numbers thus:

- 100 < ALL {110, 120, 130, 140} is TRUE.
- 100 < ALL {90, 110, 120, 130} is FALSE.

The first statement is true because 100 is less than all of the values in the given set. The second statement is false because there exists a value (90) in this set that 100 is not less than.

Using our example database, suppose we wished to find the therapists who were administering the most expensive treatments available. We could discover this as follows:

```
SELECT DISTINCT name
FROM therapists t, administration a, treatment t1
WHERE t.thno = a.thno
AND a.refno = t1.refno
AND charge >= ALL (select charge FROM treatment);
```

giving:

```
NAME
─────

Dr Lang
```

This indicates that therapist Dr Lang is administering a treatment which is at least as expensive as all other treatments available.

Suppose we wished to find any members who had a name that preceded all names of Junior members. We could discover this as follows:

```
SELECT surname, init
FROM members
WHERE surname < ALL (SELECT surname FROM members
                     WHERE type = 'Junior');
```

giving:

```
SURNAME  INIT
───────  ────

Bandar   Z
Kent     C
Green    P
Beck     J
```

The Junior member surnames consist of the set {'Swanson', 'Sharif' and 'Sharif'}. The surnames above precede all of these.

The ANY operator takes a given value with an operation and returns 'true' when it is compared against a set of values where any of those values satisfy that operation. Thus:

```
100 < ANY {110, 120, 130, 140} is TRUE;
100 < ANY {90, 110, 130} is TRUE;
100 < ANY {60, 70, 90} is FALSE.
```

The first two sets above each contain at least one value that is greater than 100. The last set contains no such value.

The command:

```
SELECT DISTINCT name
FROM therapists t, administration a, treatment t1
WHERE t.thno = a.thno
AND t1.refno = a.refno
AND charge >= ANY (SELECT charge FROM treatment)
```

would give:

```
NAME
_____

Dr Lang
Dr Crippen
```

This represents all therapists currently administering a treatment. This is because for every treatment, there will exist at least one charge that its own charge will be greater than or equal to.

The second example command rewritten using ANY:

```
SELECT surname, init
FROM members
WHERE surname < ANY (SELECT surname FROM members
                     WHERE type = 'Junior');
```

would give:

```
SURNAME  INIT
_____  ____

Bandar   Z
Kent     C
Green    P
Sharif   O
Beck     J
Sharif   O
```

The two Sharifs now appear on the list because there exists a Junior surname ('Swanson') that they precede. Thus, the ANY operator will return their names.

A command to find all therapists currently administering a treatment could
be:

```
SELECT name
FROM therapists
WHERE thno = ANY (SELECT thno FROM administration);
```

giving:

```
NAME
_____

Dr Lang
Dr Crippen
```

The subquery retrieves the thnos of all therapists currently administering
treatments. The = ANY operator causes the outer query to return only those
therapists whose thno is equal to any of these.

ANY and ALL are somewhat redundant operators. The reader may have
noticed that the word 'could' was used for each of the given examples. This
is because they could all have been coded differently, for example:

```
SELECT name
FROM therapists t, administration a, treatment t1
WHERE t.thno = a.thno
AND a.refno = t.refno
AND charge >= (SELECT MAX(charge) FROM treatment);

SELECT surname, init
FROM members
WHERE surname < (SELECT MIN(surname) FROM members
                 WHERE type = 'Junior');

SELECT surname, init
FROM members
WHERE surname < (SELECT MAX(surname) FROM members
                 WHERE type = 'Junior');

SELECT name
FROM therapists
WHERE thno IN (SELECT thno FROM therapists);
```

It is true to say that any query involving ANY and ALL can be coded differently. ANY and ALL are usually to be avoided.

'>= ALL', '> ALL', '<= ALL' and ' <ALL' can be replaced by the use of the MAX or MIN functions as demonstrated above. In these example queries, the ALL versions cause comparisons to be made against a set of values whereas the versions using the MIN and MAX function derive a single value and use that for comparison purposes. In a large database, the ALL formulation could cause considerable performance problems.

'= ANY' is always analogous to 'IN'. However, '<> ANY' is not analogous to 'NOT IN'. The following command:

```
SELECT name
FROM therapists
WHERE name <> ANY (SELECT thno from
administration);
```

would give:

```
NAME
─────

Dr Gray
Dr Lang
Dr Crippen
```

All three rows would be returned as for each row in the THERAPISTS table there does indeed exist a thno in the subquery (thnos of all therapists administering a treatment) that does not match their thno value. A correct equivalence is guaranteed by use of '<> ALL':

```
SELECT name
FROM therapists
WHERE thno NOT IN (SELECT thno FROM
administration);
```

```
SELECT name
FROM therapists
WHERE thno <> ALL (SELECT thno FROM
administration);
```

These two queries would give the same result.

▦ 7.2 NULL values

NULL is a special value in relational databases. It is literally 'not equal to anything'. Thus the command:

```
SELECT no, surname, init
FROM members
WHERE telephone_no = NULL;
```

would return no result, despite the fact that there are two members with a null value for their telephone number. NULL fails all tests of equality. To discover those members without a telephone number, we would have to test for the literal presence of a NULL value, that is:

```
SELECT no, surname, init
FROM members
WHERE telephone_no IS NULL;
```

giving:

NO	SURNAME	INIT
6	Sharif	O
8	Shafif	O

The complementary command to find all members who do have a telephone_no would be:

```
SELECT no, surname, init
FROM members
WHERE telephone_no IS NOT NULL;
```

giving:

NO	SURNAME	INIT
1	Swanson	G
2	Yeung	F
3	Bandar	Z
4	Kent	C
5	Green	P
7	Beck	J

Again, '<> NULL' would have returned no result. NULL can be neither equal nor not equal to anything.

NULL values cannot be equal to other NULL values. If we issued the command:

```
SELECT surname, init
FROM members
WHERE telephone_no = (SELECT telephone_no FROM
members WHERE no = 6);
```

we would get no rows returned. This is because member number 6 has a NULL telephone_no. Thus no other member can have a telephone_no equal to this, even those (members 6 and 8) who do have NULL as their telephone_no.

The one situation where '= NULL' is allowed is when changing the value of a column using the UPDATE command. If member number 4 were disconnected from the telephone network, we could delete their telephone number with the command:

```
UPDATE members
SET telephone_no = NULL
WHERE no = 4;
```

NULL can be used as a literal value with INSERT commands. The following command is perfectly valid:

```
INSERT INTO members
VALUES
(9, 'R', 'Biggs', NULL, NULL);
```

The above command explicitly assigns the NULL value to the telephone_no and type columns.

In Chapter 2, we stated that it is not usually possible to narrow the width of a column once it has data within it. The use of NULL can overcome this.

Suppose we decided that the column for Members' surnames was wider than required and the system that we were using disallowed the narrowing of a column containing data. We can overcome this by setting up a temporary table to hold Members' surnames thus:

```
CREATE TABLE TEMP
  AS SELECT NO, SURNAME
  FROM MEMBERS;
```

Having saved all surname values, we can delete all the original surname values:

```
UPDATE MEMBERS
SET SURNAME = NULL;
```

As there is now no data in this column, we can reduce its width:

```
ALTER TABLE MEMBERS
MODIFY (SURNAME CHAR (12) );
```

Now we can copy back the surname values and delete the temporary table:

```
UPDATE MEMBERS
SET SURNAME = (SELECT SURNAME FROM TEMP
                WHERE TEMP.NO = MEMBERS.NO);

DROP TABLE TEMP;
```

Ordering data by columns containing NULL values is problematic. SQL/92 leaves this as implementation-specific, simply demanding that every SQL product must adopt either of the following policies:

• all nulls are to be considered to be greater than all non-null values; or
• all nulls are to be considered to be less than all non-null values.

Some SQL products go further than this and will either place non-null values at the start of an ordering sequence or at the end of an ordering sequence, regardless of whether the sequence is supposed to be in ascending or descending order.

Due to the imprecise nature of the SQL standard, no example is given of ORDER BY using NULL values.

▨ 7.3 The BETWEEN operator

Suppose we had a customer for our clinic who wished to spend anything between £200.00 and £300.00 on a treatment. We could discover the range of treatments available at that price by saying:

```
SELECT * FROM treatment
WHERE charge >= 200.00
AND charge <= 300.00
```

giving:

REFNO	DESCRIPTION	CHARGE
HT1	Minor Hair Transplant	250

The same result would be achieved with the command:

```
SELECT * FROM treatment
WHERE charge BETWEEN 200.00 AND 300.00;
```

BETWEEN conditions take the form:

```
expression_x BETWEEN expression_y AND expression_z
```

which is the logical equivalent of

```
(expression_x >= expression_y) AND (expression_x
<= expression_z).
```

BETWEEN may be negated using NOT:

```
SELECT * FROM treatment
WHERE charge NOT BETWEEN 200.00 and 300.00
```

giving:

REFNO	DESCRIPTION	CHARGE
LS1	Emergency Liposuction	100
HT2	Major Hair Transplant	500
BO1	Body Deodorization	125

The condition 'charge NOT BETWEEN 200.00 and 300.00' is the logical equivalent of 'charge < 200.00 OR charge > 300.00'. The above rows meet this condition.

The BETWEEN operator is preferable to the equivalent AND/OR formulation if an index exists over the given column. If an index existed over the column CHARGE, then a non-negated BETWEEN query would look for the lower of the given comparison values in the index and retrieve all rows via the index until the higher of the comparison values was encountered in the index. If there were no values in the given range, then no rows would be retrieved at all as there would be no entries in the index. AND/OR would require full table scans regardless of the number of rows satisfying the given condition.

■ 7.4 The LIKE operator

The LIKE operator enables tables to be queried using a 'fuzzy' string value. To find all members whose name starts with the letter 'B', we would say:

```
SELECT * FROM members
WHERE surname LIKE 'B%';
```

giving:

NO	INITS	SURNAME	TELEPHONE_NO	TYPE
2	Z	Bandar	061–257–1000	Novice
7	J	Beck	345–2131	Senior

'%' is a wildcard character, meaning 'any collection of characters'. Thus, the above command retrieves all rows whose surname begins with 'B' and is followed by any collection of characters. To find all rows whose surname ends with the letter 'n' we would say:

```
SELECT * FROM members
WHERE surname LIKE '%n';
```

giving:

NO	INITS	SURNAME	TELEPHONE_NO	TYPE
1	G	Swanson	061–247–8976	Junior
5	P	Green	689–2131	Senior

The '%' character may be used more than once to find the presence of literals within strings. For instance, all hair treatments would be found thus:

```
SELECT * FROM treatment
WHERE description LIKE '%Hair%';
```

giving:

REFNO	DESCRIPTION	CHARGE
HT1	Minor Hair Transplant	250
HT2	Major Hair Transplant	500

The '—' character tests for a specific number of characters in a string. If we wanted to retrieve all members whose names started with B and which were four letters long, we would say:

```
SELECT * FROM members
WHERE surname LIKE 'B___';
```

giving:

NO	INITS	SURNAME	TELEPHONE_NO	TYPE
7	J	Beck	345—2131	Senior

'_____' indicates 'any three characters'. Wildcards may be mixed. All members with 'n' as the penultimate letter in their name would be retrieved thus:

```
SELECT * FROM members
WHERE surname LIKE '%n_';
```

giving:

NO	INITS	SURNAME	TELEPHONE_NO	TYPE
2	F	Yeung	0987—3478	Senior
4	C	Kent	345—2131	Senior

'%n_' means 'any collection of characters, followed by the letter n, followed by one character'.

LIKE may be negated using NOT. The above command using NOT LIKE would retrieve all members not satisfying the wildcard, i.e. all the other members in the table.

▓ 7.5 The EXISTS operator

The EXISTS operator is used with subqueries. Unlike all other subquery operators, a subquery used with exists will not return a set of values.

Instead, it returns a single boolean value: true or false. This means that the outer query will only return rows that cause the subquery to evaluate to a true condition. For instance, to discover the names of clients receiving treatments, we can say:

```
SELECT name FROM clients c
WHERE EXISTS
        (SELECT * FROM administration a
         WHERE a.clno = c.clno);
```

giving:

```
NAME
_____

D Green
P Pan
```

The above query returns all names from the CLIENTS table where their CLNO can be matched with a CLNO in the ADMINISTRATION table. An informal translation of the command would be: 'Find all names in CLIENTS where it is true that the CLNO equals a CLNO in ADMINISTRATION.' Note how in order to test for this, the subquery is required to perform a join with a table from the outer query. In practice, EXISTS queries will usually contain at least one such outer reference.

The negation of this query (retrieve names of clients receiving no treatments) would be expressed thus:

```
SELECT name FROM clients c
WHERE NOT EXISTS
        (SELECT * FROM administration a
         WHERE a.clno = c.clno);
```

giving:

```
NAME
_____

JP Gettysburg
G Lightly
```

This query returns names of those clients for whom it is not true that their CLNO matches any CLNO values in the ADMINISTRATION table.

In both of these queries, we have used 'SELECT *' in the inner query. The column expression used is, in fact, irrelevant as we are looking for a truth value, not a set of column values. We could have used a literal and achieved the same result, for example:

```
SELECT name FROM clients c
WHERE EXISTS
        (SELECT 'anything' FROM administration a
        WHERE a.clno = c.clno);
```

The SQL standard states that when using EXISTS, the nested query should interpret 'SELECT *' as a literal and not effect a retrieval of all columns from a table.

EXISTS may be used in subqueries with an infinite degree of nesting. Suppose we wished to retrieve details of all treatments received by P Pan. We can query the database thus:

```
SELECT * FROM treatment t
WHERE EXISTS
        (SELECT * FROM administration a
        WHERE t.refno = a.refno
        AND EXISTS
                (SELECT * FROM clients c
                WHERE c.clno = a.clno
                AND name = 'P Pan'));
```

giving:

REFNO	DESCRIPTION	CHARGE
LS1	Emergency Liposuction	125
HT2	Major Hair Transplant	500

The above query retrieves details of all treatments where it is true that its refno matches a refno in the ADMINISTRATION table and that it is true that such rows in the ADMINISTRATION table match the clno for rows in the CLIENTS table with the name value 'P Pan'.

Let us expand the ADMINISTRATION table with an extra row thus:

CLNO	REFNO	THNO
4	HT2	2
2	BO1	3
4	LS1	3
4	BO1	1

The addition of this row (<4,BO1,1>) now means that client number 4 is now receiving treatment from all three therapists. We can discover such a fact by querying the database to retrieve the names of those clients who are receiving treatment from all therapists thus:

```
SELECT name FROM clients c
WHERE NOT EXISTS
        (SELECT * FROM therapists t
        WHERE NOT EXISTS
                (SELECT * FROM administration a
                WHERE t.thno = a.thno
                AND c.clno = a.clno));
```

giving:

```
NAME

P Pan
```

In the above query we have a double negative. The inner query checks for each therapist all clients receiving treatment and returns 'true' for any client who is receiving treatment but is not seeing them. This is achieved by the inner NOT EXISTS clause. The outer query takes all clients receiving treatment but eliminates from the result, using NOT EXISTS, all those who have been flagged by the inner query. Thus, for all clients receiving treatment, we only get the names of those for whom it is not true that there exists a therapist whom they are not seeing.

We might wish to find clients treated by the same set of therapists. A query to find clients treated by the same set of therapists as 'D Green' would be:

```
SELECT name FROM clients c1
WHERE NOT EXISTS
        (SELECT * FROM administration a1, clients c2
        WHERE a1.clno = c2.clno
```

```
                AND c2.name = 'D Green'
                AND NOT EXISTS
                        (SELECT * FROM administration a2
                        WHERE a1.thno = a2.thno
                        AND c1.clno = a2.clno));
```

giving:

```
NAME
_____

D Green
P Pan
```

This indicates that P Pan is receiving treatment from all the therapists that D Green is seeing. The subquery here narrows down the set of enquiry to just those therapist numbers pertinent to D Green. We do not need to examine the THERAPISTS table to discover this. Instead, we retrieve those rows from ADMINISTRATION that join with the CLNO for D Green in CLIENTS. We then eliminate all those from the resulting set who cannot match all the THNO values in these rows.

Simple EXISTS queries may be written using IN and NOT IN. For instance, the first example in this section could have been written:

```
SELECT name FROM clients
WHERE clno IN
        (SELECT clno FROM administration);
```

More complex EXISTS queries cannot be sensibly formulated using other operators.

▓ Summary

1. ALL and ANY operators can be used to compare a value against a set of values. They are somewhat redundant operators.
2. A column without a value is assigned the value NULL. NULL may be explicitly assigned to column values. It cannot be meaningfully compared to any other value, including itself. The interpretation of NULL values in an ORDER BY clause is not precisely defined.
3. Range values can be tested using BETWEEN.
4. Wildcard characters in strings can be tested using LIKE.

5. EXISTS is the SQL equivalent of the existential quantifier. It returns a boolean value determined by whether or not a subquery can return a row.

▨ Exercises

With reference to the Bugston Operatic Club database, write the following queries:

1. (a) Retrieve names of patrons who are not attending any shows.
   (b) Retrieve the names of patrons who are buying the cheapest tickets for the show 'Nothing On'.

   Use the ANY and ALL operators only for this question.

2. Retrieve the names of all shows that have tickets between the prices of £5.00 and £10.00, along with the categories of ticket available at these prices.

3. (a) Retrieve the names of patrons who have bought tickets for all shows.
   (b) Retrieve the names of Patrons who are attending all shows also attended by J Warren.
   (c) Retrieve the names of patrons only attending shows attended by J Warren.

8 | Security and integrity

■ 8.1 Protecting tables from other users

One of the purposes of a multi-user database system is the sharing of data between the users. SQL provides the GRANT and REVOKE commands from its Data Control Language to enable the controlled sharing of data between different table owners.

GRANT takes the following basic form:

```
GRANT privilege(s)
ON table
TO user(s);
```

Privileges include the basic data manipulation operations: SELECT, INSERT, DELETE and UPDATE. Tables can be base tables or views. The user set must be a list of user names known to the database system.

For instance, if we wished to enable a user known as RICK to retrieve data from the MEMBERS table, we would say:

```
GRANT SELECT ON MEMBERS TO RICK;
```

This enables the user RICK to retrieve any data within the MEMBERS table using the SELECT command. If we wished the user VICK to be able not only to retrieve, but also to alter data within the MEMBERS table, we would say:

```
GRANT SELECT, UPDATE
ON MEMBERS
TO VICK;
```

VICK may be able to change data in this table, but he won't be able to enter new rows or delete existing rows. To do this, we would have to say:

```
GRANT SELECT, INSERT, UPDATE, DELETE
ON MEMBERS
TO VICK;
```

A quicker way to achieve the above effect would be to say:

```
GRANT ALL ON MEMBERS TO VICK;
```

It may be the case that we do not wish another user to have privileges on an entire table, but only on parts of that table. This can be achieved in various ways.

If we wish to restrict access to a subset of rows within a table, we can simply define a view of this subset and grant access to the view. Thus the command:

```
GRANT ALL ON SENIORS TO DICK;
```

will give the user Dick access to the MEMBERS table, but only to those rows and columns within the SENIORS view.

The UPDATE privilege may be restricted to columns or sets of columns. The commands:

```
GRANT UPDATE (SURNAME, INIT)
ON MEMBERS
TO MICK;

GRANT UPDATE (TELEPHONE_NO)
ON MEMBERS
TO VICK;
```

will allow the user MICK to change the surnames and initials of members and the user VICK to change their telephone numbers.

The above commands each empower one user. A set of users can be specified thus:

```
GRANT SELECT ON THERAPISTS TO RICK, MICK, VICK,
DICK;
```

If this represents the entire community of users for a database, then the command:

```
GRANT SELECT ON THERAPISTS TO PUBLIC;
```

would achieve the same effect.

Privileges may be passed on using WITH GRANT OPTION. The command:

```
GRANT SELECT, INSERT ON TREATMENTS TO VICK
WITH GRANT OPTION;
```

not only enables the user VICK to retrieve rows from and insert new rows into the TREATMENTS table, but also to pass these privileges onto other users.

REVOKE is used for removing privileges. The command:

```
REVOKE SELECT ON THERAPISTS FROM PUBLIC;
```

will remove the SELECT privilege on THERAPISTS from all database users. The GRANT OPTION is in itself a privilege which may be REVOKEd, for example:

```
REVOKE GRANT OPTION FOR TREATMENTS FROM VICK;
```

This still leaves VICK with the SELECT and INSERT privileges on this table. He simply is not now able to pass them on to anyone else.

Difficulties can arise if we try to REVOKE privileges from a user that have been passed on. For instance, suppose VICK had issued the commands:

```
GRANT INSERT ON TREATMENT TO DICK;
GRANT INSERT ON TREATMENT TO MICK;
```

If we were now to say:

```
REVOKE INSERT ON TREATMENT FROM VICK;
```

what would be the effect on the privileges that he has passed on to DICK and VICK? We may not be aware that he has passed these privileges on. We can be more precise about this by saying:

```
REVOKE INSERT ON TREATMENT FROM VICK CASCADE;
```

This will cause all dependent privileges (i.e. those given above by VICK to DICK and MICK on TREATMENTS) to be REVOKEd as well. The command:

```
REVOKE INSERT ON TREATMENT FROM VICK RESTRICT;
```

will cause the REVOKE to fail. This is because with the RESTRICT clause, privileges may only be REVOKEd if there are no other privileges dependant on them.

Sometimes a REVOKE can be ambiguous. Suppose we had the following commands:

```
GRANT SELECT ON MEMBERS TO MICK;
GRANT SELECT ON SENIORS TO MICK;
REVOKE SELECT ON MEMBERS FROM MICK;
```

The SENIORS table is a view derived from the MEMBERS table. By removing the SELECT privilege on MEMBERS, do we intend that MICK should also lose access to the SENIORS view? We can force this to be the case by saying:

```
REVOKE SELECT ON MEMBERS FROM MICK CASCADE;
```

This will debar MICK from using any view that requires the SELECT privilege on MEMBERS. The command:

```
REVOKE SELECT ON MEMBERS FROM MICK RESTRICT;
```

will cause the REVOKE to be rejected as there is another privilege (the SELECT on SENIORS) that is dependent upon it.

As an aside, at the time of writing, few products provide the CASCADE and RESTRICT options with REVOKE.

▓ 8.2 Protecting tables from yourself

In Chapter 2, we introduced the idea of constraints in table definitions. The basic role of constraints is to preserve the integrity of a database. Here we will examine further types of constraint. Regrettably, the issue of constraint definitions was given very scant treatment in SQL/89. Much of the following section was not universally defined till SQL/92 was published, and at the time of writing is supported by very few products.

First, we will revisit the topic of key constraints.

▧ 8.2.1 Candidate key constraints

All base tables in a relational database must have a primary key that uniquely identifies every row in that table. It is possible to have other unique identifiers for a table. For instance, in our THERAPISTS table, we have a THNO column that is used as the primary key. We could also include in this table an employee number (ENO) that was unique to each therapist. We can enforce this with the UNIQUE clause:

```
ALTER TABLE THERAPISTS
ADD (ENO NUMBER UNIQUE);
```

UNIQUE means that no two rows may have the same ENO value, rendering it effectively a candidate key. By definition, a column or collection of columns declared as PRIMARY KEY are also unique.

▧ 8.2.2 Foreign key constraints

In the example databases given to date, we have used a series of foreign keys. The declarations we gave in Chapter 2 were syntactically correct but left a basic issue unresolved: what do we do about preserving 'referential integrity'.

Referential integrity is an important rule for relational databases. It concerns the use of foreign keys. Briefly, it states that every value under a foreign key column must exist as a primary key value in the table that it references. For instance, in the ADMINISTRATION table the column REFNO is a foreign key that establishes a relationship to the TREATMENTS table. Referential integrity requires that every REFNO in ADMINISTRATION must also exist as a primary key REFNO value in TREATMENTS. This ensures that clients are only receiving treatments that actually exist. However, we may, from time to time, wish to alter or delete REFNO keys in the TREATMENTS table. For instance, we might wish to alter the REFNO for Major Hair Transplant in the TREATMENTS table. This will cause the rows in the ADMINISTRATION table that use the former REFNO to be invalid.

We might want to delete Major Hair Transplant as a TREATMENT. Again, this would leave rows in the ADMINISTRATION table that reference this treatment invalid.

When a primary key is altered or deleted and there are rows that reference it as a foreign key in other tables, there are three basic strategies that can be adopted:

- CASCADE: Any change to the primary key is also committed to any corresponding foreign key columns. For instance, if the REFNO for Major Hair Transplant is changed from HT2 to HT3, then all rows in the ADMINISTRATION table with the value HT2 for REFNO have that value changed to HT3. If Major Hair Transplant is deleted from the TREATMENTS table, then all rows that reference it in the ADMINIS-TRATION table are also removed.
- RESTRICT: This is effectively the opposite to CASCADE. This debars any alterations to or deletions of a primary key value if there are any rows currently referencing is as a foreign key. Thus, removing or altering the REFNO for Major Hair Transplant would not be allowed as it is currently being referenced from the ADMINISTRATION table. However, Minor Hair Transplant could be altered or removed as there are no rows anywhere in the database that are currently referencing it.

  (As an aside, SQL/92 actually uses the NO ACTION clause to specify this effect. The few SQL products that do support this feature tend to use RESTRICT. At the time of writing, RESTRICT is proposed for the next SQL standard. The difference between NO ACTION and RESTRICT is quite subtle and need not concern the reader at this point as they have the same final effect.)
- NULL: This requires that when a primary key value is changed or deleted, any foreign key references to it should be set to NULL. Thus, removing or altering the REFNO value for Major Hair Transplant will cause every row in the ADMINISTRATION table that references this treatment to have its REFNO value set to NULL.

We can specify the above when declaring foreign keys. For instance, suppose we wished, when defining the ADMINISTRATION table, that we wanted to enforce the following constraints:

- When a treatment has its REFNO changed, then all references to that REFNO must also be changed (CASCADE the UPDATE).

- When a treatment is removed, then all rows that reference that treatment must be removed (CASCADE the DELETE).

We enforce these first two constraints by the following foreign key declaration:

```
FOREIGN KEY (REFNO)
REFERENCES TREATMENTS
ON UPDATE CASCADE
ON DELETE CASCADE
```

- A patient may not have their CLNO changed if they are receiving any treatments (RESTRICT the UPDATE).
- When a client leaves, all treatments they receive are deleted (CASCADE the DELETE).

These constraints are enforced by the declaration:

```
FOREIGN KEY (CLNO)
REFERENCES CLIENTS
ON UPDATE RESTRICT
ON DELETE CASCADE
```

- When a therapist has their THNO changed, then all rows referencing them must have their THNO changed (CASCADE the UPDATE).
- If a therapist leaves, then any rows referencing that therapist must have their THNO set to NULL.

These last two constraints are enforced by the declaration:

```
FOREIGN KEY (THNO)
REFERENCES THERAPISTS
ON UPDATE CASCADE
ON DELETE SET NULL
```

Thus, the full CREATE TABLE command for ADMINISTRATION would look like this:

```
CREATE TABLE ADMINISTRATION
(CLNO NUMBER NOT NULL,
REFNO CHAR(3) NOT NULL,
THNO NUMBER,
    PRIMARY KEY (CLNO, REFNO),
    FOREIGN KEY (REFNO)
```

```
    REFERENCES TREATMENTS
        ON UPDATE CASCADE
        ON DELETE CASCADE,
    FOREIGN KEY (CLNO)
    REFERENCES CLIENTS
        ON UPDATE RESTRICT
        ON DELETE CASCADE
    FOREIGN KEY (THNO)
    REFERENCES THERAPISTS
        ON UPDATE CASCADE
        ON DELETE SET NULL);
```

(The alert reader may have noticed that we have no longer made THNO part of the primary key for the table. This is to enable NULL values to be entered for the THNO, enabling the last of the rules declared above to be enacted without leaving the table in an invalid condition (remember that no part of a primary key may have a NULL value). This does mean that this table is no longer capable of having the same treatment administered to a client by two different therapists.)

▨ 8.2.3 The CHECK clause

The CHECK clause can be used for specifying a condition that must be satisfied for a table or a column to be valid. It takes the form:

```
CHECK (conditional-expression)
```

where (conditional-expression) takes the form of a simple comparison of literal values, or may even involve a database retrieval. For instance, suppose we wished to disallow any treatment that cost more than £50,000. We could assert this as follows:

```
CREATE TABLE TREATMENTS
(REFNO NUMBER PRIMARY KEY NOT NULL,
DESCRIPTION CHAR (40),
CHARGE NUMBER (8, 2),
CHECK (CHARGE <= 50000.00));
```

Any attempts to insert charges of more than £50,000 or update existing charges to be above this value will now be rejected. This is an example of a simple comparison of literal values. Sometimes we may wish to examine the database to check the validity of a column. Suppose we wished to have a rule in the Lacrosse Club that novice members are not allowed to be selected for matches. We could enforce this by specifying a CHECK clause in the AVAILABLE table thus:

```
CREATE TABLE AVAILABLE
      (NO NUMBER NOT NULL REFERENCES MEMBERS
            CHECK (NO NOT IN (SELECT NO FROM members
                                  WHERE type = 'Novice')),
      DAY CHAR (10) NOT NULL ,
      PRIMARY KEY (NO, DAY) );
```

CHECK clauses may combine conditions using AND and OR operators. For instance, we may wish to only allow certain types of treatment (e.g. Organ Transplants) to cost more than $50,000. We could specify this as follows:

```
CHECK (CHARGE <= 50000.00 OR DESCRIPTION LIKE
'%Transplant');
```

This states that for each row in TREATMENTS, either the CHARGE value is not greater than £50,000 or the DESCRIPTION is Transplant. Any row contravening this (i.e. charges of more than £50,000 for non-Transplant treatments) will be rejected.

▓ 8.2.4 Adding or dropping constraints

Constraints may be added to a table after its initial creation by use of the ALTER TABLE command, for example:

```
ALTER TABLE TREATMENTS
ADD CHECK (CHARGE <= 50000.00 OR DESCRIPTION =
'Transplant');
```

When defining constraints, it is good practice to name them, for example:

```
CREATE TABLE AVAILABLE
(NO NUMBER NOT NULL
      CONSTRAINT no_novices
      CHECK (NO NOT IN (SELECT NO FROM members
                        WHERE type = 'Novice')),
DAY NOT NULL,
```

```
CONSTRAINT available_PK PRIMARY KEY (NO,DAY),
CONSTRAINT available_FK FOREIGN KEY (NO)
REFERENCES MEMBERS
                        ON DELETE CASCADE
                        ON UPDATE CASCADE );


ALTER TABLE AVAILABLE
ADD CONSTRAINT day_restriction CHECK (DAY IN
('Friday', 'Saturday', 'Sunday'));
```

The second of these declarations places a restriction on the days that players are available. Having given this constraint a name, we may then remove it if we find that it is no longer applicable:

```
ALTER TABLE AVAILABLE
DROP CONSTRAINT day_restriction;
```

We could also drop the constraint on members only appearing in the AVAILABLE table if they are not novices:

```
ALTER TABLE AVAILABLE
DROP CONSTRAINT no_novices;
```

Having named the primary key constraint, we could also DROP this if we so desired. We would do this with a table whose primary key we wished to alter, taking care to add a new primary key constraint having dropped the former one. Likewise, we can drop and redefine foreign key constraints if we have named them.

■ 8.2.5 Protecting view integrity

Suppose in our database, we had a view defined as thus:

```
CREATE VIEW CHEAP_TREATMENTS
AS SELECT * FROM TREATMENTS
WHERE CHARGE < 200.00;
```

Using the example data, the contents of this view would be thus:

```
CHEAP_TREATMENTS
REF DESCRIPTION                    CHARGE
___ _____               _____

LS1 Emergency Liposuction          125
BO1 Body Deodorization             100
```

This view is updateable as it is derived from only one table. The following command would therefore be valid:

```
UPDATE CHEAP_TREATMENTS
SET CHARGE = 250.00
WHERE REF = 'LS1';
```

However, this would have the effect of removing the row LS1 from the view. This is because it no longer satisfies the defining condition (CHARGE < 200.00). The following command would also be accepted:

```
INSERT INTO CHEAP_TREATMENTS
VALUES ('LA1','Leg Shortening', 1000.00);
```

This is allowed as it does not contradict any of the data type definitions for the underlying TREATMENTS table. However, it does contradict the view definition. Moreover, this row also would not be displayed through the view even though it was inserted via the view because it does not satisfy the view definition.

We can avoid these anomalies by giving a different definition:

```
CREATE VIEW CHEAP_TREATMENTS
AS SELECT * FROM TREATMENTS
WHERE CHARGE < 200.00
WITH CHECK OPTION;
```

The clause WITH CHECK OPTION means that all UPDATES and INSERTS will be checked for consistency with the view definition. Any command that contradicts the definition will be rejected. Thus the two commands above would both be rejected.

Summary

1. Tables may be shared between different database users by use of the GRANT and REVOKE commands.
2. Alternate candidate keys may be declared for tables using the UNIQUE clause.
3. Referential integrity between database tables can be maintained by use of the CASCADE, RESTRICT and SET TO NULL clauses when declaring foreign keys.
4. The CHECK clause may be used to maintain table and column integrity.
5. Integrity constraints may be named, dropped and redefined.

Exercises

Using the Bugston Operatic Club database:

1. There are three users of this database: MANAGER, BOX_OFFICE and PROMOTER. Initially, all tables belong to the MANAGER. Write the commands to achieve the following:
   (a) MANAGER gives the BOX_OFFICE the ability to retrieve, alter, remove and create new rows in the reservations table.
   (b) MANAGER gives everyone the ability to retrieve data from the SHOWS and PATRONS tables.
   (c) MANAGER give PROMOTER the ability to change and create new rows in the PATRONS table.
   (d) MANAGER gives BOX_OFFICE the ability to retrieve, alter, remove and create new rows in the TICKETS table. Furthermore, MANAGER gives BOX_OFFICE the facility to pass on these privileges.
   (e) BOX_OFFICE gives PROMOTER the ability to retrieve and create new rows in the TICKETS table.
   (f) MANAGER decides to remove the ability to create new rows in TICKETS from BOX_OFFICE and from anyone to whom BOX_OFFICE has passed this on.
2. Write new CREATE TABLE commands to enforce the following integrity rules:
   (a) In the TICKETS table, when a show has had its reference number changed, all reference numbers for the corresponding tickets must be changed. When a show is deleted, all tickets for that show must be deleted.

(b) In the TICKETS table, all tickets must be less than £20.00.

(c) Remove constraint (b) and replace it by a constraint that states that only Circle tickets may be any price; all others must be less than £20.00.

(d) In the RESERVATIONS table, when a patron is deleted, their corresponding NO is set to null. If a client has their NO altered, then their reservation number must also be altered.

(e) A show may not be cancelled or have its reference number altered if there are any reservations for that show.

(f) K Earnshaw is not allowed to reserve any tickets for the show 'From Hair to Eternity'.

9 Embedding SQL

This chapter examines the use of SQL within a 'standard' procedural programming language such as C, Pascal, FORTRAN, COBOL, Ada, etc. Prior knowledge of a language of this type is assumed. Readers without any experience of using such a language are advised to miss this chapter. The specific examples given are of using C with SQL, but they should be simple enough to make sense to any experienced programmer. I should also point out that the programs presented here are in a slightly simplified form regarding the C language. All products that provide an SQL/host language interface tend to 'ease' the use of the interface by providing some implementation-specific extensions to the given language. Such product-defined extensions have been omitted from this text.

9.1 When SQL alone is not enough

SQL/92 is not a computationally complete language. SQL is a language that is specifically designed for a limited purpose: the provision of access to data in a relational database. It does have some features that allow for the processing and formatting of such data, but it is not possible to develop complete application programs in SQL alone. Rather, SQL exists as an interface to relational databases which can then be embedded into a wide variety of applications.

The SQL standards define means by which data may be passed between SQL code and application code written in another language, known as the 'host' language. As explained in Chapter 1, this can be done in two ways: either by means of parameterized SQL modules or by directly embedding SQL code into the application code. The latter method is by far the most commonly used and will be described in this chapter.

Whichever method is used, the problem of SQL code conversion exists. Code written in a particular application language will have a compiler or interpreter associated with it which converts the language source code into machine object code, having checked that the source code complies with the syntax rules of the language. Any SQL code will be immediately rejected as not conforming to the syntax of the host language. This problem is circumvented by the use of precompilers. A precompiler takes a source program consisting of a mixture of SQL and host language statements and translates the SQL commands into statements in the host language. As with a standard compiler, the precompiler will raise errors if it cannot success-fully complete this translation. Such errors will be errors in the SQL code and errors in the use of the host language/SQL interface. Errors in the use of the host language itself will not be detected at this stage. After successful precompilation, the resulting program will still require a full compilation using the host language compiler. The process of generating application programs with embedded SQL code is illustrated in Fig. 9.1.

As stated above, most SQL/host language interface packages provide extensions to the host language. This is to render interface problems such as the mapping between host language data types and SQL data types easier to resolve. For example, in the example programs given below, the string handling would, in fact, require some extra coding in order to work reliably. An additional task for a given precompiler is to detect those parts of the original source file that consist of such implementation-specific extensions and to convert them into the standard language syntax.

▓ 9.2 Using SQL with another language

▓ 9.2.1 Host variables

Host variables are the key to communication between a host program and an SQL code segment. They are declared in the host language and shared with the SQL code. Figure 9.2 is an example of host variable use in a C program.

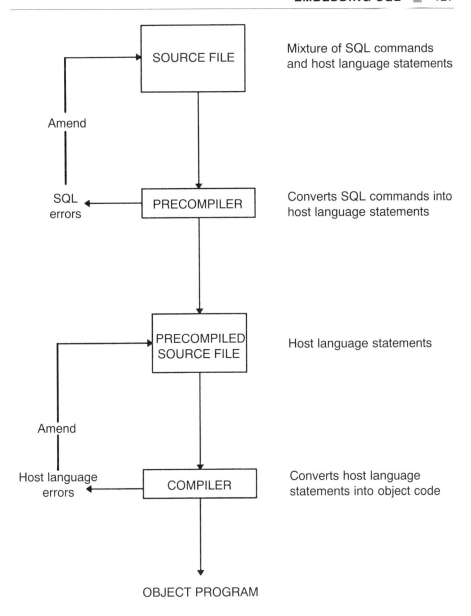

Fig. 9.1 The SQL Pre-compilation Process

This is not yet a syntactically correct piece of code. However, it introduces certain features of the standard SQL/host interface.

At the start of the program, we have the declaration of the host language variables 'name' and 'no'. We will use these to access the MEMBERS table

```
char *name;
int no;

main()
{
 printf("Enter number of member to be retrieved: ");
  scanf("%s", &no);
      SELECT name
      INTO :name
      FROM members
      WHERE members.no=:no;
  printf("\n Name of member is: %s",name);
  exit(0);
}
```

Fig. 9.2 The use of Host Variables

on member no and retrieve their name. The host language then prompts the user for a member no value. This is then followed by a form of the SQL SELECT command that is rather different to that encountered before in this text:

```
SELECT name
INTO : name
FROM members
WHERE no =:no;
```

In this command we use column names from the database (name, no) and host variable references (:name,:no). We distinguish between the two by placing a colon (':') before any host variable reference. In this way, data can be passed from a host program into an SQL command and passed from an SQL command into a host program.

Note the use of the INTO clause. This is required by all embedded SQL SELECT commands. This transfers data retrieved from a table column into a host variable. The data type of the host variable must be compatible with that of the column. This is one of the things that the precompiler will check for.

As already stated, this is not yet a syntactically correct program. The precompiler is only able to check SQL statements and the use of the SQL/host language interface. In order to do this, it must have some means of distinguishing host variable declarations from other declarations and SQL commands from host language statements.

▨ 9.2.3 The EXEC SQL command

EXEC SQL is used to indicate to the precompiler those parts of a program which it must check and attempt to translate into host language code. In Fig. 9.3, we have inserted EXEC SQL statements at the appropriate points.

At the start of the program, we now have the statement 'EXEC SQL BEGIN DECLARE SECTION;'. This tells the precompiler that what now follows is a set of host variable declarations. This is terminated by the command 'EXEC SQL END DECLARE SECTION;'. Any data declarations made after this point are purely local to the host language and may not be referenced by any embedded SQL commands. Thus the SQL command itself is now prefixed by the 'EXEC SQL' command. This alerts the precompiler to check the correctness of the succeeding SELECT command. As with direct SQL, all embedded SQL commands are terminated with a semicolon. The

```
EXEC SQL BEGIN DECLARE SECTION;
   char *name
   int no;
EXEC SQL END DECLARE SECTION;

main()
{
  printf("Enter number of member to be retrieved: ");
  scanf("%s", &no);
  EXEC SQL SELECT name
      INTO :name
      FROM members
      WHERE members.no=:no;
  printf("\n Name of member is : %s", name);
  exit(0);
}
```

Fig. 9.3 The use of EXEC SQL statements

precompiler will ignore anything that comes after the semicolon until it next encounters an EXEC SQL command.

▓ 9.2.4 Exception handling and error trapping

The program in Fig 9.3 would still not satisfy a precompiler thatconforms to the SQL standard as it has no provision for dealing with thenumerous error or exceptional situations that can arise when interfacing a host language to a relational database. All embedded SQL programs must include the standard variables 'sqlstat' and/or 'sqlcode'. These return status codes which can be used to provide information on the state of the database/ programmatic interface.

For instance, 'sqlcode' is a signed integer. A value of 0 for sqlcode indicates that no error situation exists. A value of 100 indicates a retrieval operation that has returned no rows. Other positive values indicate a warning. A negative value for sqlcode indicates an error has occurred when accessing the database.

We could rewrite this program as shown in Fig. 9.4.

Although syntactically correct, this code segment has a number of problems, not least being the fact that 'sqlcode' is a 'deprecated' standard. This means that it is earmarked for removal from the standard. Programmers should instead use the 'sqlstate' variable which has a more precisely defined set of values. (Most 'sqlcode' values are implementation-specific whereas most 'sqlstate' values are standard defined.) Although the 'sqlstate' value set is more precisely defined, it is still subject to revision and extension. Because of this transitory state of the standard, a number of precompilers provide an SQLCA ('SQL Call Area') file which contains all of the required data declarations for error and exception handling.

The program also has a number of 'if' statements to test status values. This can be done in a more elegant form using the WHENEVER command. WHENEVER has the following syntax:

```
WHENEVER { SQLERROR | NOT FOUND }
         { CONTINUE | GOTO | STOP }
```

This means that WHENEVER can detect any of the following conditions:

```
EXEC SQL BEGIN DECLARE SECTION;
   char *name;
   int no;
   int sqlcode;
EXEC SQL END DECLARE SECTION;

main()
{
  printf("Enter number of member to be retrieved: ");
   scanf("%s", &no);
   EXEC SQL SELECT name
      INTO :name
      FROM members
      WHERE members.no = :no;
   if (sqlcode < 0)
    {printf " \n Fatal error has occured");
    exit(1);
    }
   if (sqlcode = 0)
    printf("\n Name of member is: %s", name);
   if (sqlcode = 100)
    printf("\n No members with this number");

exit(0);
}
```

Fig. 9.4 Use of the 'sqlcode' status flag

- SQLERROR: this means that a potentially fatal error has occurred during the execution of an SQL command;
- NOT FOUND: an SQL retrieval operation has failed to retrieve any rows.

For each of these conditions, an appropriate action may be taken:

- CONTINUE: attempt to execute the next statement in the program;
- GOTO: pass control to another part of the program;
- STOP: terminate the program. With certain implementations, a different command may be required, e.g. BREAK, QUIT, etc.

The program in Fig. 9.4 should be rewritten as shown in Fig 9.5.

```
EXEC SQL BEGIN DECLARE SECTION;
   char *name;
   int no
exec sql end declare section;

EXEC SQL INCLUDE SQLCA;

main()
{
  printf("Enter number of member to be retrieved: ");
   scanf("%s", &no);

   EXEC SQL WHENEVER NOT FOUND GOTO no_one;
   EXEC SQL WHENEVER SQLERROE STOP;

   EXEC SQL SELECT name
      INTO :name
      FROM members
      WHERE members.no=:no;
   printf("\n Name of member is: %s", name);
   exit(0);

no_one:
   printf("\n No member with that number");
   exit(1);
```

Fig. 9.5 Use of the WHENEVER flag

The statement INCLUDE SQLCA directs the precompiler to import the file by this name containing all data declarations required by the SQL standard. (The provision of such a file saves the programmer a lot of effort and reduces their potential for making errors!)

The WHENEVER statements at the start of the program act as a global definition of what action to take in certain situations. Here we have simply instructed the program to terminate if an error situation arises. We could instead have directed control to a subroutine that tested the 'sqlstate' or 'sqlcode' value and given an appropriate message. The second WHEN-EVER declaration flags the situation in which no record is found to match the given user input. In this case, control is passed to a separate part of the program.

Programs that contain a number of SQL commands may require exceptions to be handled in different ways according to the command used. This is easily accounted for. WHENEVER commands may be given on multiple occasions in a program. Each time an SQL command is executed, if an error condition occurs then the most recently entered WHENEVER command will take effect. We shall see examples of this later.

9.2.5 CONNECTing to a database

The above program could raise a runtime error. This is because it assumes that some sort of connection has been made to a database. However, this may not be the case. To make a database connection, the CONNECT command must be used.

CONNECT takes the following form:

```
CONNECT [TO] { DEFAULT | literal }
```

DEFAULT indicates that the program will attempt to connect to the system-defined default SQL database, if one exists. 'literal' is used to define a specific database. The way that a particular database is specified is implementation-dependent. Different SQL products will use their own methods of locating a database, these methods themselves sometimes varying according to the platform used.

In this text we will use the simplest case where a database may be identified by a single string, e.g. 'members'. Thus, the program given above with an explicit CONNECT command would look like Fig. 9.6.

9.2.6 Updating a database with embedded calls

The program above performs a simple SELECT command. The full range of SQL commands may be used in an embedded program, including data definition commands as well as data manipulation commands. Figure 9.7 is an example of a program that prompts a user for values for new records, alterations to existing records and deletions of existing records. In this program we make multiple declarations of WHENEVER conditions.

```
EXEC SQL BEGIN DECLARE SECTION;
char *database;
char *name;
int no;
EXEC SQL END DECLARE SECTION;

EXEC SQL INCLUDE SQLCA;

main()
{
  printf("Enter number of member to be retrieved: ");
    scanf("%s", &no);
    strcpy (database, 'members');

    EXEC SQL WHENEVER NOT FOUND GOTO no_one;
    EXEC SQL WHENEVER SQLERROR STOP;

    EXEC SQL CONNECT :database;

    EXEC SQL SELECT name
        INTO :name
        FROM members
        WHERE members.no=:no;
    printf("\n Name of member is: %s",name);
    exit(0)

no_one:
    printf("\n No member with that number");
    exit(1);
}
```

Fig. 9.6 Connecting to a Database

In Fig. 9.7, the SQL command COMMIT WORK has been used. This command makes permanent any database operations enacted during the course of a program. Without this command, alterations to the database will be lost on termination of the program. The user dialogue in these examples is in itself quite terse. A realistic program would take the opportunity to validate and check the user input and, hopefully, present a more friendly interface to the database.

```
    EXEC SQL WHENEVER NOT FOUND GOTO update not_found;
    EXEC SQL WHENEVER SQLERROR GOTO update_error;
    EXEC SQL SELECT init,surname,type
    INTO :init, :surname, :type
    WHERE no = :no;
    printf ("Current type is: " );
    printf ("\n", type);
    printf ("Please enter new type :");
    scanf ("%s", type);
    EXEC SQL UPDATE MEMBERS SET type = :type
    WHERE no = :no;
    EXEC SQL COMMIT WORK;
    printf ("Update successfully completed \n");
        goto end_update;
update_not_found: printf("No member with this
  number \n");
    goto end_update;
update_error: printf ("Update failed due to database
  error \n");
end_update: printf ("End of update \n")
}
delete()
{
    printf("Enter No of Member to Delete :");
    scanf("%d", &no);
    EXEC SQL WHENEVER NOT FOUND GOTO delete_not_found;
    EXEC SQL WHENEVER SQLERROR GOTO delete_error;
    EXEC SQL DELETE FROM MEMBERS
    WHERE no = :no;
    EXEC SQL COMMIT WORK;
    printf ("Deletion successfully completed \n");
    goto end_delete;
delete_not_found: printf("No member with this
  number \n");
            goto end_delete;
delete_error: printf ("Delete failed due to database
  error \n");
end_delete: printf ("End of delete \n");
}
```

Fig. 9.7 Using the full range of DML commands in a program

```
#include <stdio.h>

EXEC SQL BEGIN DECLARE SECTION
  char *database;
  int no;
  char *init;
  char *surname;
  char *telephone no;
  char *type;
EXEC SQL END DECLARE SECTION;

EXEC SQL INCLUDE SQLCA;

EXEC SQL DECLARE memb CURSOR FOR
SELECT init, surname, telephone no
FROM members
WHERE type = :type
ORDER BY surname;

main()
{ strcpy (database, 'members');
  EXEC SQL CONNECT :database;

  printf ("Please enter type of member to be
   retrieved: ");
  scanf ("%s", type);

  EXEC SQL WHENEVER NOT FOUND GOTO end_loop;
  EXEC SQL WHENEVER SQLERROR GOTO end_loop;

  EXEC SQL OPEN memb;

  for(;;)
  {
      EXEC SQL FETCH memb INTO
      :init,:surname,:telephone_no;
      printf("%-4s%-20s%-12s\n" ,init,surname, telephone_no);
  }
end_loop: EXEC SQL WHENEVER SQLERROR CONTINUE;
   EXEC SQL COMMIT WORK;
   EXEC SQL CLOSE memb;
}
```

Fig. 9.8 Use of a CURSOR for multiple row retrieval

▨ 9.2.7 Multiple row retrievals

All of the examples given above demonstrate embedded SQL operations using a single row retrieved from a database. SQL SELECT commands frequently retrieve sets of rows, with the size of the set being infinitely variable. This causes a problem with standard procedural languages which can only work on a 'record at a time' basis. This is overcome by the use of a CURSOR.

A CURSOR is a program variable associated with a SELECT command. When the command is executed, the cursor acts as a pointer moving down the set of rows retrieved, returning them one at a time. In order to process such a set of rows, the host program must set up a loop which makes successive calls of the cursor until no more rows are retrieved. There are four EXEC SQL commands associated with cursors:

DECLARE CURSOR: specifies the command to be associated with a given cursor, for example:

```
DECLARE CURSOR C1 FOR SELECT refno, description, charge
                     FROM treatments;
```

Cursors may be declared in any part of a program. Note that there is no INTO line in a cursor declaration. Database values are bound to host variables at a later point. The same cursor can be used at different program points to retrieve data into different host variables. Host variables may be referenced in the WHERE clause of a cursor in order that a host variable value may be used to access the database.

- OPEN CURSOR: starts an instance of a cursor, for example:

    ```
    OPEN CURSOR C1;
    ```

    At this point, no data is yet returned by the cursor. It is simply 'ready for use'.
- FETCH: brings cursor data into given host variables, for example:

    ```
    FETCH C1 INTO:refno,:description,:charge;
    ```

- CLOSE CURSOR: closes a cursor. Failure to close a cursor before its next use (i.e. its next OPEN) will result in an error situation.

Fig 9.8 is a program that retrieves and displays all members of a type entered by the user, with the output displayed in surname order:

In this program we have set up an infinite loop that fetches and displays data from the database. The WHENEVER NOT FOUND declaration instructs the program to jump beyond the loop. NOT FOUND will be activated if there are no members matching the type entered by the user or at the point when the cursor has finished going through the set of rows retrieved by the command and has no more to fetch. This particular program makes no effort to trap errors.

▓ Summary

1. SQL commands may be embedded into a host language by use of an SQL pre-compiler.
2. Embedded SQL commands are prefixed by the phrase 'EXEC SQL'.
3. Communication between a host language and an embedded SQL command is through host variables which are specially declared in an SQL declaration section.
4. Error trapping and special conditions are detected by use of the EXEC SQL WHENEVER command.
5. Multiple row select commands require the use of a cursor.

▓ Exercises

1. Using a programming language of your choice, write a program with embedded SQL commands that retrieves details of all types of tickets and their associated prices for a given show in the Bugston Operatic Club database. The name of the show is to be entered by the user.
2. Extend this program so that the user is given the choice to change the price of a given ticket type, with the new price being written directly to the database.
3. Extend this program further so that when an alteration is made to a ticket price, details of all reservations affected by this change, including the name of the patron, are displayed. These details should have the following columns:

```
NameofPatron PreviousCostofReservation NewCostofReservation
```

10 Advanced SQL

In this chapter we shall outline features of the SQL/92 standard that are seldom supported by existing products but which will hopefully become commonplace within the next few years.

■ 10.1 User-defined domains

Every column in a relational database table has a data type which draws its values from a given domain. SQL provides a limited range of primitive data types (INTEGER, FLOAT, CHAR, etc.). With the majority of SQL products, this is all that is supported along with, occasionally, a small set of product-specific primitives. The SQL/92 standard allows for the creation of user-defined domains with the CREATE DOMAIN command. With this command, the user can name a domain and define its data type in terms of existing primitives. Once declared, this domain can be used as a data type in a CREATE TABLE command.

For example, we could define a domain 'DAYS' thus:

```
CREATE DOMAIN days CHAR (9);
```

and then use it in a CREATE TABLE commmand:

```
CREATE TABLE available
    (NO NUMBER,
    DAY DAYS,
    PRIMARY KEY (NO, DAY));
```

A more precise definition of a domain can be achieved by use of a constraint clause, for example:

```
CREATE DOMAIN days CHAR(9)
      CONSTRAINT DAY_CONSTRAINT
      CHECK (VALUE IN ('Monday', 'Tuesday',
                       'Wednesday', 'Thursday',
                       'Friday', 'Saturday',
                       'Sunday'));
```

This means that any column value whose data type is 'DAYS' must be a string of not more than nine characters and that this string must be from the restricted set specified by the above CHECK clause. In this example, the CHECK clause uses the word 'VALUE' to test the value of a domain item. VALUE is a reserved word in SQL which may only be used when defining a domain constraint.

Constraints may be added or dropped using the ALTER DOMAIN command, for example:

```
CREATE DOMAIN client_name CHAR (20);
```

```
ALTER DOMAIN client_name
      ADD CONSTRAINT lords
      CHECK (VALUE LIKE 'Lord%');
```

The above commands create a domain 'client_name' which is then constrained so that all client_name values must start with the string 'Lord'. If this is found to be not useful, we can drop this constraint:

```
ALTER DOMAIN client_name
      DROP CONSTRAINT lords;
```

Default values can also be specified, for example:

```
CREATE DOMAIN patient_status CHAR (8)
      DEFAULT 'Live';
```

If we now use this domain in a table definition, it has an implication for INSERT commands on this table. Take the following commands:

```
CREATE TABLE patients
(PNO NUMBER NOT NULL PRIMARY KEY,
PNAME CHAR (30),
STATUS patient_status);

INSERT INTO patients VALUES (1,'P Smith');
```

The effect of the above commands will be to create a row in the table PATIENTS with the values <1,'P Smith','Live'>. This is despite the fact that the INSERT command gave no value for the STATUS column. However, because the STATUS column has the user-defined data type 'patient_status', the associated default value 'Live' has been assigned in the absence of any given value.

Default values may also be altered and dropped using ALTER DOMAIN:

```
ALTER DOMAIN patient_status
SET DEFAULT = 'Still Alive';

ALTER DOMAIN patient_status
DROP DEFAULT;
```

Domains may also be dropped:

```
DROP DOMAIN patient_status;
```

When a domain is dropped, columns that are defined on this domain have their data type altered to the primitive data type on which the domain was originally defined. All constraints associated with that domain are exported to the base table definitions of columns defined for that domain.

A more precise version of DROP DOMAIN is:

```
DROP DOMAIN CASCADE/RESTRICT;
```

With this version, the CASCADE option has the effect described in the paragraph above. RESTRICT means that the DROP will fail if there are any columns in the database using this domain as their data type.

The title of this section is a little misleading. A true domain not only consists of a range of data values, but also has a range of operations that can be performed on such values. There is no facility in SQL/92 for user-defined operations on domains. This topic is under examination for the next version of SQL. The only operations that can be performed on SQL/92 domains are those associated with the base data type on which the domain was defined. There is additionally no facility for defining domains based on user-defined domains.

▩ 10.2 Database integrity through assertions

CREATE DOMAIN allows constraints to be placed upon all columns with a given data type. The CREATE ASSERTION command allows constraints of an arbitrary complexity to be defined upon an abitrary set of columns and tables. These can be thought of as 'general' database constraints.

For instance, suppose we wished to ensure that we only had clients for our clinic that were also members of the Lacrosse Club. We can specify this as follows using the NOT EXISTS operator over the relevant tables:

```
CREATE ASSERTION members_only
    CHECK (NOT EXISTS (SELECT * FROM clients
    WHERE name NOT IN (SELECT inits||surname
    FROM members) );
```

This means that any attempt to insert a row into the CLIENTS table whose name does not exist in the MEMBERS table will be rejected by the system. Also, any attempt to update a client's name to one that does not exist in the MEMBERS table will fail.

If we wished to extend this assertion such that we prohibit clients who have the same name as a therapist, we would say:

```
CREATE ASSERTION members_only_no_therapists
   CHECK (NOT EXISTS (SELECT * FROM clients
        WHERE name NOT IN (SELECT init||surname
                            FROM members)
          OR name IN (SELECT name FROM therapists)));
```

The effect of the above will be that any attempt to insert or update a row in any of the relevant tables (THERAPISTS, MEMBERS, CLIENTS) that leads to a contradiction of this assertion will fail. The first part of this command is, in fact, redundant as it already exists as part of a previous assertion.

Here is a constraint to check that no one is receiving a set of treatments whose total cost exceeds £1,000,000:

```
CREATE ASSERTION check_bill
    CHECK (NOT EXISTS (SELECT * FROM clients c
                    WHERE 1,000,000 <
                        (SELECT SUM(CHARGE)
                        FROM admin a, treatment t
                        WHERE a.refno = t.refno
                        AND a.refno = c.refno)));
```

The above command checks that there does not exist any client for whom it is true that 1,000,000 is less than the sum of all their treatment charges.

Assertions can be dropped:

```
DROP ASSERTION members_only;
```

■ 10.3 The JOIN expression

JOIN can be used to build table expressions. For instance, the command:

```
SELECT DISTINCT name
FROM therapists NATURAL JOIN administration;
```

has the same effect as:

```
SELECT DISTINCT name
FROM therapists, administration
WHERE therapists.thno = administration.thno;
```

NATURAL JOIN creates a table derived from the join of two tables using whichever columns are common to both tables. A JOIN expression across a series of tables will be nested thus:

```
SELECT * FROM therapists NATURAL JOIN
                (clients NATURAL JOIN
                        (treatment NATURAL JOIN
                        administration));
```

This causes ADMINISTRATION to be joined with TREATMENT. The result of this is joined with CLIENTS. The result of this second join is then joined with THERAPISTS, returning a join of all four tables.

This is nearly the equivalent of:

```
SELECT * FROM
therapists t, clients c, treatment t1,
administration a
WHERE t.thno = a.thno
AND c.clno = a.clno
AND t1.refno = a.refno;
```

The equivalence is not quite true because when using NATURAL JOIN, the column that is common to both tables is only returned once. The second of the above statements will replicate those columns that are common to more than one table.

Replicated columns would appear with the following expression:

```
SELECT * FROM
members JOIN available ON members.no =
available.no;
```

The ON clause would usually be used when a join is desired over two tables without common columns or if a join based on inequality was desired.

All of the joins described in the text up to this point have been 'inner joins'. These are joins that return all rows from two or more tables that satisfy a given join condition. An 'outer join' is one that additionally returns rows from any tables that do not satisfy the given condition. An example of an outer join would be to return clients and administration details, including clients receiving no treatment:

```
SELECT * FROM
clients FULL NATURAL JOIN administration;
```

giving:

CLNO	NAME	THNO	REFNO
1	JP Gettysburg		
3	G Lightly		
2	D Green	3	BO1
4	P Pan	2	HT2
4	P Pan	3	LS1

In addition to three rows that satisfy the join we now also have two rows for the two clients who are receiving no treatments and thus do not satisfy the join. This is achieved by use of the FULL option.

Outer joins can also be specified using LEFT and RIGHT. The clause 'T1 LEFT NATURAL JOIN T2' will return rows from table T1 which will not satisfy the join, but not from T2. 'T1 RIGHT NATURAL JOIN T2' will return rows from table T2 which do not satisfy the join, but not from T1. 'T1 FULL NATURAL JOIN T2' will return all rows from both tables that cannot perform the join.

▨ 10.4 The CASE expression

CASE can be used to return a value on one of a specified set of conditions. It takes the form:

```
CASE [ WHEN condition THEN expression ] ...
        [ELSE expression]
END
```

It can be useful with update commands, for example:

```
UPDATE members
SET telephone_no = (CASE WHEN type = 'Novice' THEN
                              '897—1234'
                        WHEN type = 'Senior' THEN
                              '345678'
                  ELSE  (SELECT telephone_no FROM
                        members WHERE no = 1)
                  END);
```

The above command has the effect of setting all Novice telephone numbers in the members table to '897–1234', all Seniors to '345678' and all others to the same number as that assigned to member number 1.

▓ Summary

1. User-defined domains may be created from base data types in SQL. These place simple restrictions on the set of values that can be assigned to a column.
2. Constraints across a database may be defined using the CREATE ASSERTION command.
3. The JOIN expression may be used to join tables. Variants of this expression may be used to achieve various forms of outer join.
4. Commands with a conditional element may be written using CASE.

▓ Exercises

1. Create a domain for the Bugston Operatic Society that restricts names of patrons to strings of 30 characters. Call this domain 'Names'.
2. Create a domain that can be used for the price of tickets that limits the maximum charge for a ticket to £999.99. Call this domain 'Ticket_Price'.
3. Write an assertion that ensures that no patron can reserve tickets with a value of more than £10,000.00.
4. Using the JOIN expression:
   (a) Write a query that returns, for each booking made, the details of the patron, the details of the show and the details of the ticket.
   (b) Rewrite (a) so that it also returns details of any patron that has not made any bookings.
   (c) Rewrite (b) so that it also returns details of any shows for which a booking has not been made.

11 | Future SQL

In this chapter we shall look at a range of possible future directions for SQL. These include some of the features currently proposed for the next version of the standard ('SQL/3') as well as research-based proposals for extending SQL into application areas where relational databases have as yet had little impact, such as spatial databasesystems and active databases.

11.1 SQL/3 proposals

In this section, we shall outline some of the possible extensions that will appear in the next SQL standard.

11.1.1 Primitive data types

It is proposed in SQL/3 that the data types BOOLEAN and ENUMERATED be added to the current range of available primitives. Thus one could have the following CREATE TABLE command:

```
CREATE TABLE guides
(NO NUMBER NOT NULL PRIMARY KEY,
NAME CHAR (20),
MUSIC BOOLEAN,
SWIMMING BOOLEAN,
BOOK_LOVER BOOLEAN,
EXPLORER BOOLEAN
RANK ENUMERATED ('Junior', 'Senior', 'Leader') );
```

The above is a table for a set of guides with a column for each badge that they might be awarded. They also have a rank value which is represented by one of an ordered list of string literals. This allows for commands such as:

```
INSERT INTO guides
VALUES (1, 'J Smith', FALSE, TRUE, FALSE, FALSE,
'Junior');

UPDATE guides
SET swimming = TRUE
WHERE name = 'M Ngugih';

SELECT * FROM guides
WHERE explorer;
```

The first of these commands creates a row for a Junior guide who has the swimming badge but no others. The second command sets all guides with the name 'N Ngugih' to have a swimming badge. The third command finds all guides for whom it is true that they have the explorer badge.

The enumerated type (RANK) allows for commands such as:

```
SELECT * FROM guides
WHERE rank < 'Leader';
```

▦ 11.1.2 Universal quantifiers

It is proposed for SQL/3 that the quantifiers 'FOR ALL' and 'FOR SOME' be included with the following data types:

```
FOR {SOME | ALL} table_expression (conditional
expression);
```

The FOR SOME quantifier is equivalent to the THERE EXISTS quantifier from standard predicate calculus. It returns the value TRUE if there is anything within a given set of values that satisfies a given constraint. For instance, a command to retrieve names of clients who are receiving treatment:

```
SELECT * FROM clients c
WHERE FOR SOME (SELECT * FROM administration a)
(a.clno = c.clno);
```

This instructs the system to return rows from the CLIENTS for whom it is true that there exists a row in the ADMINISTRATION table that has a matching CLNO value. A command to retrieve clients receiving all treatments would be:

```
SELECT name FROM clients c
WHERE FOR ALL (SELECT * FROM treatment)
              (refno IN (SELECT refno
                         FROM clients NATURAL JOIN
                              administration x
                         WHERE x.clno = c.clno));
```

The above command retrieves, for each client, the set of 'refno' values for treatments that they are receiving. The outer query returns the name of that client if it is true that every 'refno' in TREATMENTS exists in the set of refnos for that client. This means that they must be receiving all available treatments. Intuitively, this is a much simpler way to express this query than in the example given in Chapter 7 using the EXISTS operator.

▨ 11.1.3 Role-based security

In SQL/92, there is only one grouping of users for security purposes, the group PUBLIC meaning 'all other current users'. SQL/3 proposes the facility for system-defined groups in order that users may be assigned to groups according to their 'role' and privileges granted according to their role.

For instance, we might wish to create a role 'BROWSER':

```
CREATE ROLL BROWSER;
```

We could then assign a number of users to this role, for example

```
GRANT BROWSER TO MICK, VICK, DICK, RICK;
```

We can then grant a privilege to this entire set of users thus:

```
GRANT SELECT ON TREATMENT TO BROWSER;
```

Similarly, we can remove privileges from this group:

```
REVOKE SELECT ON THERAPISTS FROM BROWSER;
```

The command:

```
REVOKE BROWSER FROM MICK;
```

will have the effect of removing all privileges associated with that group from the user MICK.

■ 11.1.4 User-defined functions

This is a natural enhancement of user-defined domains.

Suppose we wished to have a domain that stored coordinates for plotting points on a diagram. Values in such a domain would require two real numbers representing the 'x, y' values of a location on a two-dimensional plane. We would need to define a domain thus:

```
CREATE DOMAIN POINT REP (X FLOAT, Y FLOAT);
```

The above command creates a domain 'POINT'. Each value in this domain is represented by two real numbers. The word REP stands for 'INTERNAL REPRESENTATION'. We can now use this domain when creating tables, for example:

```
CREATE TABLE TRIANGLES
      (TID NUMBER PRIMARY KEY NOT NULL,
      A POINT,
      B POINT,
      C POINT);
```

This creates a table named 'Triangles' where each row has three columns (A, B, C) of data type POINT. In order to insert and retrieve data from this table, we need to define some functions for this domain:

```
CREATE FUNCTION MAKEPOINT (A FLOAT, B FLOAT): (POINT)
  AS
    DECLARE P POINT;
    P.X:= A;
    P.Y:= B;
    RETURN (P)
END;


CREATE FUNCTION X (P POINT): (FLOAT)
  AS
    RETURN (P.X)
END;
```

The first of these functions takes two real numbers and creates a POINT type object from these, with the two reals assigned to the x and y coordinates of this object. The second takes a POINT type object and returns the x coordinate of this point.

We can now use these functions thus:

```
INSERT INTO triangles
VALUES
(1, MAKEPOINT(11.1, 12.2), MAKEPOINT (6.5, 4.3),
MAKEPOINT (8.8, 9.7) );
```

This creates a triangle with the given coordinates for each point, using the MAKEPOINT function to convert the given numbers into data of type POINT.

To find any two triangles whose first point starts at the same 'X' coordinate, we would say:

```
SELECT * FROM triangles A, triangles B
WHERE X(A.A) = X(B.A)
        AND A.TID < B.TID;
```

This uses the 'X' function to return the x coordinate for POINT A of each triangle.

The function declarations above make use of procedural code in order to define their effect. Procedural coding facilities such as blocks, loops, assignments and conditional statements are proposed for SQL/3 in order that it may become a computationally complete language.

The ability to define functions upon domains also provides the SQL user with the ability to build what are, in effect, user-defined abstract data types.

▓ 11.2 Non-relational applications of SQL

In this section, we shall briefly outline extensions to SQL that take it away from the purely relational context. Much of this only really exists as a research item and is by no means 'standardised' or 'stable'. Indeed, most of what is described here is still the subject of much controversy and debate.

A list of richly referenced texts is given at the end for the reader who may wish to study any of these topics further.

■ 11.2.1 Inheritance

Inheritance is a concept developed mainly in the object-oriented paradigm. Briefly, it is the process whereby an object type (or 'class') may inherit all of the characteristics of another type of object. An inheritance chain in a relational database would enable one relation to inherit the attributes of another. A form of implementation in SQL could be thus:

```
CREATE TABLE PERSON
     (FNAME CHAR (30),
     LNAME CHAR (30),
     STREET CHAR (30),
     CITY CHAR (10),
     DATE_OF_BIRTH DATE,
     GENDER {F,M} );

CREATE TABLE EMP ISA (PERSON)
     (NATINSID CHAR (10) UNIQUE,
     WORKSNO    NUMBER NOT NULL,
     GRADE NUMBER,
     DEPARTMENT CHAR (5)
     PRIMARY KEY (WORKSNO) );
```

In the example above, EMP is defined 'ISA (PERSON)', meaning that all rows in the table EMP have the attributes that are described for the table PERSON. Any user-defined functions for the data types of these attributes would be inherited. If we have specialized forms of EMP, we could create a further table, for example:

```
CREATE TABLE MANAGER ISA (EMP)
     (PERSONAL_ASSISTANT NUMBER REFERENCES EMP,
     FUNCTIONAL_RESPONSIBILITY CHAR (10) );
```

This states that a MANAGER inherits all of the attributes of an EMP, but has a couple of additional attributes. WORKSNO as their primary key will have been inherited. This could be redefined by a fresh declaration of primary key for MANAGER.

Domain inheritance could also be implemented. Suppose we had a domain declared thus:

```
CREATE DOMAIN PARALLELOGRAM
REP (A POINT, B POINT, C POINT, D POINT)
CHECK (ANGLE(A, B, C)=ANGLE(A, D, C) AND
ANGLE(B, A, D)=ANGLE(B, C, D));
```

This defines a figure with four points with the opposing angles of those four points being equal, rendering it a parallelogram. (This depends on the existence of a user-defined function 'ANGLE'.) We could then define a domain rectangle as a type of parallelogram:

```
CREATE DOMAIN RECTANGLE ISA (PARALLELOGRAM)
CHECK (ANGLE(A, B, C) = 90));
```

This constrains rectangles to be parallelograms with the starting corner to be 90 degrees. This means all corners will be 90 degrees. All other attributes of the parallelogram will be inherited along with all functions defined on parallelograms. We might have defined a function to calculate areas for parallelograms thus:

```
CREATE FUNCTION AREA (P PARALLELOGRAM): (FLOAT)
AS
      DECLARE A, B, C, D, X, Y: POINT;
      REC: FLOAT;

      A := P.A; B := P.B; C := P.C; D := P.D;
      IF ANGLE(A, B, C) < 90
            ANGLE(B, X, A):=90;
            ANGLE(D, Y, C):=90;
            REC :=(LEN(A, X)* LEN(X, C))
      ELSE
            ANGLE(A, X, B):=90;
            ANGLE(C, Y, D):=90;
            REC :=(LEN(B, X)* LEN(B, Y));
      END-IF;
      RETURN ((0.5*LEN(B, X)* LEN(A, X))+(0.5 *
            LEN(D, Y)* LEN(C, Y))+ REC);
   END;
```

This divides the parallelogram into two right-angled triangles and a rectangle and returns the sum of the three areas. This would not be appropriate for rectangles. We could redefine for rectangles thus:

```
CREATE FUNCTION AREA (R: RECTANGLE): (FLOAT);
AS
RETURN (LEN(R.A, R.B)* LEN(R.B, R.C))
END;
```

Any domains that are inherited from rectangle (such as a domain for squares) will now automatically inherit this function rather than the one defined for parallelograms.

In SQL/3, there exist proposals for the definition of 'subtables' that can inherit the proprties of 'supertables'.

▓ 11.2.2 Object-based SQL

Abstract data typing and inheritance provide relational domains with the main features associated with the object-oriented paradigm. This hints at a certain rapprochement between relational database technology and object-oriented database technology. There are some systems that implicitly propose a merger of these technologies by way of implementing an 'object-oriented' version of SQL. Such systems usually propose the replacement of table definition by 'type' definition, a 'type' being analagous to an object 'class' with an associated set of methods (which are broadly analagous to the functions decribed above) and an inheritance mechanism. Data is inserted into the database by creating instances of a type.

One such system is IRIS, which, briefly, consists of an object manager over a relational database. Certain syntactic changes are made to the SQL, which is retitled 'Object SQL' (OSQL). What follows is a highly-edited form of OSQL.

Examples of type creation (as opposed to table definition) in OSQL as follows:

```
CREATE TYPE DEPT
      (DEPTNO STRING REQUIRED UNIQUE,
      DEPTNAME STRING UNIQUE);
```

```
CREATE TYPE EMP
     (EMPNO INTEGER REQUIRED UNIQUE,
     EMPNAME STRING,
     BELONGS_TO DEPT);
```

The second declaration establishes a relationship between an EMP and a DEPT, stating that the 'BELONGS_TO' attribute of an employee object indicates a DEPT type object. To populate this database, we need to instantiate (create instances of) these object types:

```
CREATE DEPT (DEPTNO, DEPTNAME)
     INSTANCES accounts (1, 'Accounts'),
               sales (2, 'Sales');


CREATE EMP (EMPNO, EMPNAME, DEPTNAME(BELONGS_TO))
     INSTANCES smith (1, 'Smith', 'Accounts'),
               jones (2, 'Jones', 'Sales');
```

The second of the commands above indicates that the property DEPTNAME is being used to identify the department that an employee belongs to. With each instance, we have assigned an identifier (accounts, sales, smith, jones). In an object database, every object must have a unique identifier which never changes. This is different to a primary key value in a relational database, which may change for a given row.

We can define functions in order to implement methods for a type. For instance, a method to return the set of employees for a given department may be defined as:

```
CREATE FUNCTION employed_by (Dept d)  →  SET OF emp
     AS
     SELECT EACH emp e
     WHERE d IN belongs_to(e);
```

This function returns the set of EMP objects which have the given DEPT object as their BELONGS_TO property. We can now use this function in a query thus:

```
SELECT empname(employed_by(d))
FOR EACH dept d
WHERE deptname = 'Planning';
```

The above command examines the current set of DEPT objects and for each one whose deptname is 'Planning' the function employed_by is called to return the set of employees employed by that department. EMPNAME is called on this function to return the name of each employee returned.

Functions can also be used to nest sets within an object. For instance, a set of skills for an employee could be built thus:

```
CREATE FUNCTION has_skill(emp) —— SET OF string;
```

We can supply a set of skills or add to a set using this function:

```
SET has_skill(jones) = {'Pascal','SQL','IEW'}
ADD has_skill(smith) = {'SQL'}
```

Retrieval of all employees with the SQL skill would be:

```
SELECT empname
FOR EACH emp e
WHERE 'SQL' IN has_skill(e);
```

▓ 11.2.3 Temporal SQL

A temporal database is one that captures information regarding the state of data through time. Much of the research in temporal SQL has been devoted to extending the data types and operations in order that time information can be included in a relational database.

With a temporal database, we could record information about the times of operations in our Health Clinic thus:

```
OPERATIONS
CLNO    REFNO    THNO    SCHEDULE            THEATRE
────    ─────    ────    ─────────           ───────

2       BO1      3       19.00  –  21.00     2
4       HT2      3       18.00  –  20.00     3
```

In this table, the SCHEDULE column will have a 'TIME' data type which can be tested using special operators. For instance, to find whether the same therapist is booked into two theatres at the same time:

```
SELECT * FROM operations a, operations b
WHERE a.thno = b.thno
      when a.schedule overlaps b.schedule
      and a.theatre < b.theatre;
```

The temporal operator 'overlaps' is used to check whether there is any time common to to any two schedules involving the same therapist in different theatres. This is prefixed by the 'when' clause, meaning the comparison returns 'true' when a time overlap occurs. Other possible temporal operators proposed include 'before', 'after', 'during', 'follows' and 'precedes'.

At the time of writing, temporal database technology is still an emerging area and there is yet to appear a single well-accepted temporal version of SQL.

▨ 11.2.4 Active SQL

Classic relational databases consist of passive data which alters its state as a result of explicit operations on that data. An active database is one where the data 'reacts' to operations. For instance, a query on one table may cause other tables to be queried in order that a correct response may be given. An update to one table may cause a series of operations on other tables to be performed. Foreign key integrity constraints and the CREATE ASSERTION command are examples from the current standard of an 'active' form of SQL whereby actions on one table may trigger events on other tables. The CREATE TRIGGER command is proposed for SQL/3 whereby actions on one table may trigger or be constrainned by actions on another.

For instance, suppose we had two tables, EMP indicating the employees in a firm and DEPT indicating the departments in a firm with a foreign key (DNO) linking each employee to a department. We might have an integrity constraint stating that a department row in DEPT may not be deleted if it is referenced by any employee rows in EMP. We might wish to override this for departments with less than ten employees. We can define a trigger to do this as follows:

```
CREATE TRIGGER Dept_Del
BEFORE DELETE ON DEPARTMENT d
WHEN 10 > (SELECT COUNT(*) FROM EMP WHERE EMP.DNO
          = d.DNo)
    DELETE EMP WHERE EMP.DNO = d.DNO;
```

The above trigger checks for employees belonging to departments with less than 10 members. Such employees are deleted before the relevant row is deleted from the DEPT table, thus avoiding any foreign key constraint conflicts. Events can also be triggered after an action using ON rather than BEFORE.

Much research is presently being conducted into 'intelligent' databases. An intelligent (or 'deductive') database has two components: data and rules. The data part is the equivalent of the base tables of a relational database. Rules can be applied to this data to 'derive' what is known as an 'intensional' database. A different set of rules will give a different intensional database. The same rules applied to a different set of base data will give a different intensional database. Rules themselves may be shared between different systems.

One approach to implementing such a system is to extend SQL to inlude the definition of rules as well as tables. Such rules can be used to derive complex information from the database and also to trigger events based on a detailed evaluation of database information. For instance, the credit-worthiness of a customer could be specified thus:

```
CREDIT_WORTHY;
DELETE FROM Credit_Worthy;
FOR ALL
    SELECT *
    FROM Customers C
    WHERE Credit_Limit > (SELECT SUM(Total_Cost)
                          FROM Invoices I
                          WHERE I.Cno = C.Cno)
    AND NOT EXISTS (SELECT * FROM Bad_Debts B
                WHERE B.Cno = C.Cno)
DO
    INSERT INTO Credit_Worthy (C.Cno)
END;
```

This rule consists of two conditions that have to be satisfied before the given action (inserting a given customer number into a table of credit worthiness) can take place. The DO part may consist of a series of actions, some of which may in themselves call in rules.

▪ 11.2.5 Spatial SQL

Spatial databases have been receiving considerable attention in recent years. A spatial database is one that contains data that pertains to the space occupied by data objects. They are vital for applications such as computer-aided design, image databases, geographical databases, engineering systems and so on. A number of extensions to SQL and the relational model itself have been proposed in order that the convenience, elegance and power of relational technology may be be applied to the field of spatial databases. There do also exist some products that provide an SQL type language for a spatial database.

A spatial form of SQL requires, minimally, a range of spatial data types and associated operations and, preferably, the facility for user-defined spatial objects. Whereas classic SQL deals with tables, a spatial SQL must deal with graphical representations of spatial objects. The declaration of spatial objects takes the form of a table declaration using a mixture of standard and spatial data types, for example:

```
CREATE TABLE roads
(road_id number NOT NULL PRIMARY KEY,
road_name CHAR(30),
road_type CHAR(30),
road_coords LINE_SEGMENT);

CREATE TABLE regions
(region_id NOT NULL PRIMARY KEY,
region_name CHAR(30),
region_type CHAR (30),
region_location REGION);
```

The above tables both make use of a spatial data type: LINE_SEGMENT to plot the path of a road on a map and REGION to plot the boundaries of a region. This reflects the fact that two different roads may cross paths and two different regions may overlap. We could constrain certain types of region from overlapping, for example:

```
CREATE ASSERTION admin_regions
CHECK (NOT EXISTS (SELECT * FROM regions r,
                   regions r1
                   WHERE OVERLAPS (r.region_location,
                   r1.region_location)
                   and r.region_id != r1.region_id
                   and r.region_type = 'Local
                   Government'));
```

This constrains all 'Local Government' regions to occupy a distinct space.

We may then have queries such as:

```
SELECT * FROM roads, regions
WHERE INTERSECT (road_coords, region_location)
AND region_name = 'North West';

SELECT * FROM roads, regions
WHERE road_type = 'Motorway'
AND region_type = 'Local Government';
```

The first query returns a map of all roads within regions named 'North West'. The second returns a map of all motorways in all local government regions.

▓ Summary

This chapter has been a 'cook's tour' of probable future directions for SQL. It is neither comprehensive nor complete in its coverage, and cannot be so in the space allowed. The intention has been to give a brief flavour of the main developments in the language, many of which are still far from stable.

▓ Bibliography

Abiteboul, S., Hull, R. and Vianu, V. (1995) *Foundations of Databases*, Addison-Wesley.

Beynon-Davies, P. (1991) *Expert Database Systems*, McGraw-Hill.

Brown, A. (1992) *Object Oriented Databases: Applications in Software Engineering*, McGraw-Hill.

Date, C.J. (1995) *An Introduction to Database Systems*, 6th edn, Addison-Wesley.

Date, C.J. and Darwen, H. (1993) *A Guide to the SQL Standard*, 3rd edn, Addison-Wesley.

Hughes, J. (1991) *Object Oriented Databases*, Prentice-Hall.

W. Kim, (ed.) (1995) *Modern Database Management*, Addison-Wesley.

Tansel, A.U., Clifford, J., Gadia, S., Jajodia, S., Segev, A., and Snodgrass, R. (1993) *Temporal Databases – Theory, Design and Implementation*, Benjamin/Cummings Publishing.

Appendix
SQL syntax summary

The syntax summary provided here is relatively informal and simplified. It consists of a series of SQL command definitions. The symbols used are as follows:

Symbol	Meaning
`:: =`	'defined as'
`CAPITALS`	indicates an SQL reserved word
`{ }`	indicates those words or phrases that are a compulsory part of a definition
`[ ]`	indicates those words or phrases that are an optional part of a definition
`|`	indicates a choice of words or phrases
`...`	placed at the end of a word or phrase which may be repeated

Where a word is undefined (e.g. 'tablename'), this means that it can be substituted by a literal.

▓ A.1 SQL Data definition

```
create_table_command:: =
      CREATE TABLE tablename
      { (column_specification | table_constraint
      [, column_specification | table_constraint ...])
      | [AS select_command] };
```

```
column_specification:: =

  column_name { data_type | domain_name }
  [column_constraint ...]
```

```
data_type:: =

    CHAR (string_width)
  | NUMBER [(num_width[,precision]]
  | FLOAT [(num_width[,precision]]
  | INTEGER
```

```
column_constraint:: =

    {NULL | NOT NULL} [CONSTRAINT constraint_name]
  | {UNIQUE | PRIMARY KEY} [CONSTRAINT constraint_name]
  | foreign_key_specification [CONSTRAINT constraint_name]
  | check_specification [CONSTRAINT constraint_name]
```

```
table_constraint:: =

  {UNIQUE | PRIMARY KEY} (column [,column ... ] )
    [CONSTRAINT constraint_name]
  | FOREIGN KEY (column[,column ... ])
  foreign_key_specification
    [CONSTRAINT constraint_name]
  | check_specification [CONSTRAINT constraint_name]
```

```
foreign_key_specification:: =

  REFERENCES tablename [(column[,column ... ])]
  [ON DELETE referential_action]
  [ON UPDATE referential_action]
```

```
referential_action:: =

  CASCADE | SET NULL | RESTRICT | NO ACTION
```

```
check_specification:: =

  CHECK (conditional_expression)

create_view_command:: =

  CREATE VIEW viewname [column_alias [,column_alias ...]]
  AS
  select_command
  [WITH CHECK OPTION];

alter_table_command:: =

    ALTER TABLE tablename
    {ADD (column_specification | table_constraint)
  | MODIFY (column_specification)
  | DROP CONSTRAINT constraint_name};

create_assertion_command:: =

  CREATE ASSERTION assertion_name
     check_specification;

create_domain_command:: =

  CREATE DOMAIN domain_name
  [ AS ] data_type
  [ DEFAULT {literal | NULL} ]
  [ check_specification [CONSTRAINT constraint_name] ];

alter_domain_command:: =

  ALTER DOMAIN domain_name
    {ADD check_specification [CONSTRAINT constraint_name]
  | DROP CONSTRAINT constraint_name
  | SET DEFAULT {literal | NULL}
  | DROP DEFAULT};

create_index_command:: =

  CREATE [UNIQUE] INDEX
     indexname
     ON table (column [,column ... ] );

drop_table_command:: =
```

```
DROP TABLE tablename
    [ RESTRICT | CASCADE ];

drop_view_command:: =

  DROP VIEW viewname
    [ RESTRICT | CASCADE ];

drop_assertion_command:: =

  DROP ASSERTION assertion_name;

drop_domain_command:: =

  DROP DOMAIN domain_name
  [ RESTRICT | CASCADE ];

drop_index_command:: =

  DROP INDEX indexname;
```

▨ A.2 SQL data manipulation

▨ A.2.1 Data retrieval commands

```
table_expression:: =

    select_command
  | join_table_expression

select_command:: =

  SELECT [ ALL | DISTINCT] select_item_list
  FROM table_ref [,table_ref ...]
  [WHERE conditional_expression]
  [GROUP BY column_ref [,column_ref ...]]
  [HAVING conditional_expression] ]
  [ {UNION | INTERSECT | EXCEPT } table_expression ]
  [ORDER BY order_by_clause];

select_item_list:: =

   *
  | scalar_expression [AS alias] [,scalar_expression
  [AS alias] ... ];
```

```
table_ref:: =

    tablename [ [AS] range_variable]
  | join_table_expression
  | (table_ref) [AS range_variable]

join_table_expression:: =

  table_ref [NATURAL] [join_type] JOIN
  { table_ref | ( join_table_expression) }

join_type:: =

    INNER
  | LEFT [OUTER]
  | RIGHT [OUTER]
  | FULL [OUTER]
  | UNION

order_by_clause:: =

  {column_ref | integer} [ASC | DESC]
  [, order_by_clause ... ]

select_into_command:: =

  SELECT [ALL | DISTINCT] select_item_list
  INTO host_variable_list
  [WHERE conditional_expression]
  [GROUP BY column_ref [,column_ref ... ] ]
  [HAVING conditional_expression];

host_variable_list:: =

  host_variable [,host_variable ...]

cursor_declaration:: =

  DECLARE CURSOR cursorname
  CURSOR FOR table_expression;

open_cursor_command:: =

  OPEN cursorname

fetch_command:: =
```

```
FETCH cursorname INTO host_variable_list;
```

close_cursor_command:: =

```
CLOSE cursorname;
```

■ A.2.2 Data alteration commands

insert_command:: =

```
INSERT INTO tablename
[column [,column ... ]
{VALUES (literal [,literal ... ]) | table_expression};
```

update_command:: =

```
UPDATE tablename
SET {column_ref_list | select_ref_list}
[WHERE conditional_expression];
```

column_ref_list:: =

```
column = {scalar_expression |
NULL}[,column_ref_list ... ]
```

select_ref_list:: =

```
column [,column ...] = table_expression
```

delete_command:: =

```
DELETE FROM tablename
[WHERE conditional_expression];
```

■ A.3 SQL data control

grant_command:: =

```
GRANT privilege [,privilege ...] ON object
TO grantee [,grantee ... ]
[WITH GRANT OPTION];
```

grantee:: =

```
  username
| PUBLIC
```

```
privilege:: =

    SELECT
  | UPDATE
  | DELETE
  | INSERT
  | ALL

object:: =

    tablename
  | DOMAIN domain_name

  revoke_command:: =

  REVOKE privilege [, privilege ...] ON object
  FROM grantee [,grantee ... ]
  {RESTRICT | CASCADE};
```

▦ A.4 Miscellaneous

```
conditional_expression:: =

  [NOT] { scalar_expression { = | != | < | > | <= |
  < > | >= } scalar_expression
   | scalar_expression [NOT] BETWEEN
     scalar_expression AND scalar_expression
   | character_string_expression [NOT] LIKE string_spec
  | scalar_expression IS [NOT] NULL
  | scalar_expression {= | != | < | > | = | = } {ANY
  | ALL }
    (table_expression)
  | scalar_expression [NOT] IN (table_expression)
  | IS [NOT] {TRUE | FALSE | UNKNOWN }
  | UNIQUE (table_expression)
  | EXISTS (table_expression) }
    [{AND | OR} {conditional_expression} ...]

string_spec:: =

  '{string_literal | comparator}[{string_literal |
  comparator} ...]'
```

```
comparator:: =

  % | _[_ ...]

scalar_expression:: =

  numeric_expression |
  character_string_expression

numeric_expression:: =

  numeric_primary |
  numeric_expression { + | - | * | / } numeric_primary

numeric_primary:: =

  column_ref
  | numeric_literal
  | aggregate_function
  | (table_expression)
  | (numeric_expression)

character_string_expression:: =

    character_string_primary
  | concatenation_expression

character_string_primary:: =

    column_ref
  | literal
  | aggregate_function
  | (table_expression)
  | (character_string_expression)

concatenation_expression:: =

  character_string_expression ||
  character_string_primary;

column_ref:: =

  [{tablename | range_variable}.] column

aggregate_function:: =

    {SUM | AVG | MAX | MIN | COUNT}
    ([ALL | DISTINCT] scalar_expression)
  | COUNT(*)
```

Bibliography

Apart from the list given at the end of Chapter 11, the following books and papers formed the basis of this text:

ANSI Document X3.135–1986, *Database Language SQL* (defines SQL/86).

ANSI Document X3.135–1989, *Database Language SQL* (defines SQL/89).

ANSI Document X3.135–1992, *Database Language SQL* (defines SQL/92).

ANSI Document X3.168–1989, *Database Language Embedded SQL* (defines embedded SQL).

Codd, E.F. (1990) 'A relational model for large shared data banks', *Communications of the ACM*, Vol. 13, No. 6.

Codd, E.F. (1990) *The Relational Model for Database Management*, Addison-Wesley.

Date, C.J. (1995) *An Introduction to Database Systems*, 6th edn, Addison-Wesley.

Date, C.J. and Darwen, H. (1993) *A Guide to the SQL Standard*, 3rd edn, Addison-Wesley.

Date, C.J. and White, C.J. (1992) *A Guide to DB2*, 4th edn, Addison-Wesley.

Elmasri, R. and Navathe, S.B. (1994) *Fundamentals of Database Systems*, 2nd edn, Addison-Wesley.

Rolland, F.D (1991) *Relational Database Management with ORACLE*, 2nd edn, Addison-Wesley.

Van Der Lans, R.F. (1993) *Introduction to SQL*, 2nd edn, Addison-Wesley.

Where possible, all code in this text has been tested on a Unix platform using an ORACLE database system running SQL*Plus. The following manuals were used:

ORACLE SQL Language Reference Manual, Part No. 778-V6.0.
*ORACLE Pro*C User's Guide*, Part No. 3504-V1.1.
Programmer's Guide to the ORACLE Precompilers, Part No. 5315-V1.3.

Index